REA

Lying Together

Lying Together

My Russian Affair

Jennifer Beth Cohen

THE UNIVERSITY OF WISCONSIN PRESS
TERRACE BOOKS

The University of Wisconsin Press
1930 Monroe Street
Madison, Wisconsin 53711

www.wisc.edu/wisconsinpress/

3 Henrietta Street
London WC2E 8LU, England

1   3   5   4   2

Printed in the United States of America

Library of Congress Cataloging-in-Publication Data
Cohen, Jennifer Beth.
Lying together: my Russian affair / Jennifer Beth Cohen.
p.   cm.
ISBN 0-299-20100-7 (cloth: alk. paper)
1. Cohen, Jennifer Beth.   2. Cohen, Jennifer Beth—Relations with men.
3. Foreign correspondents—United States—Biography.
4. Journalists—United States—Biography.   I. Title.
PN4874.C635A3   2004
070.4′332′092—dc22   2004005255

Terrace Books, a division of the University of Wisconsin Press, takes its name
from the Memorial Union Terrace, located at the University of Wisconsin–Madison.
Since its inception in 1907, the Wisconsin Union has provided a venue for
students, faculty, staff, and alumni to debate art, music, politics, and the issues of the day.
It is a place where theater, music, drama, dance, outdoor activities,
and major speakers are made available to the campus and the community.
To learn more about the Union, visit www.union.wisc.edu.

FOR MY FAMILY

Author's Note

In the interest of privacy and respect, many names of people and institutions that appear in this book have been changed. In the interest of a smoother narrative, I have slightly shifted some time frames, and some characters are composites. I have also disguised details about other characters to safeguard their privacy. But this is a true story. I know that, because it is my story.

I

OVER THE ATLANTIC—"Are you afraid of flying?" my seatmate asks me. He is frantically chewing gum, and the scent of synthetic spearmint is hovering, stalled around my head. I try to snuff it out by shoving my nose into the pages of a book, but he will have none of it. He asks again. Reluctantly, I turn toward him, and it occurs to me that I should feel fortunate to be seated next to this chatty, bloated, balding man. "Elder John," says the enamel name tag pinned to his cardigan. A Mormon missionary, the kind that have been swarming to Russia like drunks to a vodka kiosk at the beginning of the day. Except the missionaries seem to think that they are going to be able to control the chaos, not get lost in it. Their arrogance annoys me, and normally I would sooner sit on the wing of the plane than next to this man. But given the situation, I decide to take it as a possible sign from heaven that my aisle partner is a direct conduit to the divine himself.

"No, why?" I say, offering a painfully large smile.

"I can hear your heart pounding from over here," he says.

"Oh, God," I say, quickly regretting my choice of words. But he doesn't seem to mind. He tilts his head with an encouraging nod.

"My fiancé is meeting me in St. Petersburg," I say in that slightly maniacal tone one uses when speaking more to vent nerves than thoughts.

"You haven't seen him for awhile?" says the missionary. It's a really personal question, to be sure, but his is a comforting tone. The way he asks it blows an air of calm over me and I take no offense. It feels a bit like I'm sitting inside one of those idealized Catholic confessional scenes you see on television, the ones where the priest calls the sinner "my child" in a deep, warm, and encouraging timbre while the checkered pattern of the dividing screen creates a delicate and slightly sexy shadow on the star's face. It works magic on me, because, whether he knows it or not, part of me is a nasty sinner just dying to repent.

"Six years," I say.

Forgive me, Father, for I have sinned. It has been six years since I last laid eyes on the man I plan to marry. I have rejected the advice of my friends and family and chosen to go with my gut, Father.

"I haven't seen him since we studied Russian in college together," I add. "Just e-mails and phone calls. Just this past month." I wait to gauge his reaction, but he doesn't have much of one, aside from another encouraging tilt. So I continue. "Well, we aren't really engaged, not officially, but we've talked about it and everything." I pause. "You are probably thinking it's like one of those mail-order bride scenarios but in reverse or something?" My head is bobbing up and down like a chimp's in a zoo. Nerves.

"No, not at all," he says, sounding something like God himself.

"Right. I mean, that's not really what I meant, but it's odd, I know. I mean, most of my friends think I'm nuts," I say, thinking I both look and sound completely nuts. My sister-in-law gave me the pink silk scarf that I now have tied around my neck to lend me a bit of a Jackie O. flair when I step off the plane. My family has been tentative at best about this romance, and the scarf seemed a bit of an olive branch. So did the matching sunglasses my mother bought for me, the ones that are now precariously resting on the top of my dark, disheveled hair, ready to fall into place on the bridge of my nose with a simple shake of my head.

The missionary nods gently and offers some gum. It's a substitute for brushing your teeth, he explains. Great for travel. He shows me the packaging with the larger-than-necessary seal of approval from the American Dental Association. I take a piece.

"It is a bit nuts," I continue, accidentally spitting on his sleeve. He doesn't notice. "I've really never felt so simultaneously right about something and terrified at the same time."

And then he starts to get all religious on me, preaching about God's will and fate and whatnot. It's normally stuff that would irritate me to no end. But given that I am flying 600 miles an hour into the arms of a man I have never so much as kissed, I am in no place to judge someone else's leaps of faith. And in a way, all this religiosity validates the feeling I have, this sense that I suppose most people feel when they have fallen in love, this sense that I have been blessed.

We first met at our Boston-area college during the spring of 1992. The place had a painful reputation as a safety school for Ivy League wannabes: people who reached for the top and wound up tangled on a lower rung of the ladder. In the world of Upper Middle Class Urbanites from which I sprung, it was a pretty fair assessment. But a sprinkling of brilliant minds and eccentric thinkers was to be found there, and I was lucky enough to find a fair share of them.

It was the last semester of my senior year, and I signed up for independent study with Professor Dobrak—Russian 502: The Works of Angsty Russian Writers Read in the Original, or something along those lines. He invited another student, Kevin Dillard, to join us. We bonded, the three of us, enamored of our mutual admiration for the mystical misery of Russia. I had spent two of my college summers there and was planning to return in the fall. Kevin had done his junior year in St. Petersburg and was soon setting off to study some more. And Professor Dobrak, well, he had made a life out of it.

Twice a week the three of us sat in his cramped, dusty office in Hull Hall and tried to deconstruct those great literary classics. Kevin was lanky and rumpled. I was mildly bulimic and moderately groomed. Professor Dobrak was a sad-looking fortysomething with thickly framed eyeglasses reminiscent of a Soviet apparatchik's. The seminar always ran late as we lapped up each other's anecdotes and caught up on current events. It was not six months since the Soviet Union had collapsed, and we got a kick out of trying to tie the tomes of the 1800s to the contemporary world. It was a bit like putting together a puzzle with pieces hiding under rugs. But that's the thing of it; in the front of almost every textbook on Russian history or Russian literature appears a quote from Churchill about Russia's being a riddle wrapped in a mystery inside an enigma. It is used so often that it is almost clichéd, but it does get to the heart of this fascination that most Western-blooded Russophiles feel. In my mind it was about wanting to understand the unimaginable and, by understanding, having some sort of power over or against the unpredictable. It's not that Russia is the only chaotic, endlessly entertaining entity on Earth; it's just that Russians and Russia are enough like us and our society that we can almost relate to them. Looking at them is like looking at your reflection in a fun-house mirror. The image looks like you but distorted, and in small areas sometimes it's a little more interesting. I think Kevin thought that too. From across the desk we shared knowing glances; we nodded in agreement as the other made a point.

The last day of the term, the two of us brought vodka, caviar, and black bread, and with Dobrak we practiced being "Russian." We debated the proper way to do a vodka shot. (Do you sniff the bread or eat it? Do you gulp the vodka down slowly or in one fell swoop?) Dobrak kept pouring. We tossed and tossed and drank *"do dna"*— to the bottom. All that was left at the end of the lesson were three dirty glasses and some bread crumbs scattered about the professor's wooden desk.

The next morning, for the first time in my sober college career, I had a horrible hangover. I felt giddy with my badness.

When the phone rang, I knew who it was.

We met for coffee and eggs in nearby Harvard Square. I brought Kevin an old volume of *Crime and Punishment* that I had picked up near the Hermitage the summer before. He brought me some Advil. After we ate, we strolled, our legs slow and heavy from lack of sleep and too much food. We walked across the Charles River Bridge. I had a churning feeling inside me, like a propeller winding, preparing for a great release. We talked about the future in that eager way college students tend to do, excited and hopeful. Plotting and scared. Or at least I was. Kevin seemed to be a bit more confident than everyone else. A bit fearless. Just a bit. I admired him for that, but I didn't say so. I was hoping that he thought I was a bit fearless too.

We circled the banks of the river, the Boston side, the Cambridge side, and back again. We walked until the sun was setting over the skyline, and then we stopped.

We were standing on the Harvard Bridge, studiously watching the sailboats, pretending to ignore the tension between us.

"I decided to go to Berkeley for my Ph.D.," he said.

"I know."

"You do?"

"Yeah, Dobrak told me. He seemed disappointed you wouldn't be staying in town."

"And you?"

"I won't be in town either."

I told him I was thinking of going to Moscow to do an internship with one of the news networks. Maybe I'll see you there someday, he said.

We looked at each other for a moment. Just a moment. Then he looked at his watch.

"I have to go meet Vicki," he said, referring to the woman he was living with.

"I know. My boyfriend will wonder what happened to me," I said, "I should go." And I did.

But that was more than six years ago.

To tell this story from that point, I would have to drone on about six years of failed relationships, family illnesses, a few deaths, graduate schools, career successes and failures (we both became journalists), ten countries (I wound up in New York, he in Russia), eating disorders (mine), rehab clinics (his), a broken engagement (mine), a divorce (his), and God knows how many lovers between the two of us. Life. So at risk of reducing myself to a cultural stereotype, I'll just say that by the time I hit my late twenties, I was feeling a bit like the many mildly neurotic, man-obsessed, therapy-dependent single women who were starting to populate prime-time television shows and pulp fiction. But I also had another stereotype to fall back on: I am the child of a psychiatrist and a psychotherapist, and you know what they say. They say that children of psychiatric professionals tend to be nuts. Actually, it's not entirely true. My brother is tremendously normal. Also not entirely true is the myth that the relationships between mental health professionals and their children are dysfunctional and often estranged. In my case it was just the opposite. We were overly functional and we talked about everything. So those mid-to-late twentysomething years involved a fair amount of crying to my folks, who in turn tried desperately to convince me that it would all work out fine: I would get my career in order, I would achieve great things, I would find my Prince Charming, though not necessarily in that order. It took years of therapy to figure out why, if my parents were so optimistic and encouraging, I still felt like I was a failure. The answer was simple. I thought they were lying.

I loved my parents, but I found solace in my like-minded, similarly situated friends.

My friends and I often tried to convince ourselves that we were better off not getting seriously involved with our soul mates until later in life because the longer you wait, the more you know yourself and your wants and your needs. Your emotional requirements are less compromising; you have more control. We were probably lying to ourselves on some level, but if it helped assuage the loneliness, so be it. But I wonder sometimes what destruction and chaos Kevin and I might have caused the world by now if we had tried to merge our lives back then. Or what wonders. And I wonder whether my mid-to-late twenties would have been stronger, more successful, more vibrant if we had solidified our union then and I didn't experience all the broken hearts and failed relationships that I did. Would

I have had the guts to leave my hometown and return to Russia after graduate school like I wanted to, to laugh at my mildly lucrative New York–based job offers and follow my heart? Would I have become the kind of journalist I wanted to be, instead of the one I had become? I don't know. Because we didn't merge back then and all I know is what actually did happen. Or at least I know most of what actually did happen. So I am going to skip forward a few years in the telling, to a point when twenty-eight years of bumps and scratches had made us both mature enough to recognize a risk and scared enough to take one.

I would be dishonest if I said that when I first contacted him, it was only about work. A part of me, a very conscious part (the looking for love part), was curious to check in on his marital status, his emotional status, his potentially latent interest in me. I could have chosen to hire any number of journalists I knew in Russia. I chose Kevin.

After a number of attempts at setting a tone that was somehow flirtatious and professional, I sent him this:

TO: kdillard@spbpress.ru
FROM: jcohen@breakingstory.com
DATE: January 20, 1998
RE: whoring around the globe

Hey Dillard, remember me? It's Jennifer. You know, the other party responsible for your final college hangover? Sorry I haven't been in touch for a while. But then again, neither have you. I heard you were in New York last summer visiting the latest love interest. Is she the one tattooed into your arm or is that someone else? Yes, Josh does have a big mouth. Well, if you were here, I am sorry we didn't get to see each other. But I won't take it personally. I forgot to call you last time I was in Russia. Anyway, I stumbled across your e-mail address when I was reading your paper's web site. News editor, huh? A far cry from academia, but I am very impressed. Actually, I knew to look for you there. Josh told me you have been out seeking death threats from the Russian Mafia of late (congrats on winning the Glasnost Award, by the way. Now not only will the Russian Mafia be looking to behead you, but the local Russian journalists will want you dead as well. How embarrassing to be beaten out by a smart-ass American!).

But this is why I write. I am working as an investigative producer for *Breaking Story,* a (yes, tabloid!) television magazine show here in New York and am looking into doing a story I think you might be of great assistance on. In fact, I think we'd like to hire you to help me out from that end (we pay dollars—not rubles). We are talking Russian Mafia, prostitutes, and other juicy things I shouldn't put into this e-mail in the event that the FSB is reading your files. There is information I don't want to detail until I know you are interested in working with me. Interested? Write ASAP. Let me know where and when I can call. I look forward to hearing from you.

Jen

It was hardly an hour before I got a response. Probably sometime around midnight St. Petersburg time. I know this because I had just returned from my afternoon Starbucks run, tall skim cappuccino in tow.

I sat down in my ugly but ergonomically correct tweed chair and took the plastic lid off the paper cup. A moment of serene calm in the sea of a frenzied newsroom.

I gently tickle the top layer of foam. A deep breath. I close my eyes. I open them slowly as I raise the cup to my lips. And then—

The mail flag on my computer screen pops up. Normally. I would have continued with the sip, but I was compelled to put the cup down and click on the mouse.

TO: jcohen@breakingstory.com
FROM: kdillard@spbpress.ru
DATE: January 20, 1998
RE: Re: whoring around the globe
    Hey back! So good to hear from you. Wasn't sure you had made it

back alive from Croatia (yes, Josh has a big mouth. He told me about the orange smuggling). Surprised you didn't wind up in some Serbian prison. Or did you? Still, I'm more surprised you returned from covering that war-torn hellhole. Actually, I'm surprised you aren't based here, covering this hellhole. And speaking of hellholes, I'm in the office if you want to call. 011-7-812-XXX-XXXX. Will be here for another hour. The guard answers the phone at night, and he is probably smashed on vodka, so be patient when he tries to transfer you. Or call me at home. 011-7-812-XXX-XXXX.

K

PS Different chick is written on my arm. I still have to either find another woman named Vicki or find a way to morph those letters into something else. You still dating the DC Republican Josh told me about? Or did you finally find the nice Jewish doctor you are fated to marry, the lucky bastard?

K

The latent interest was definitely not just potential. It was most definitely there. And not even that latent.

I responded immediately.

TO: kdillard@spbpress.ru
FROM: jcohen@breakingstory.com
DATE: January 20, 1998
RE: Re: Re: whoring around the globe
Actually, it was a Bosnian prison. But the guards were cute in that dark, Mediterranean, malnourished sort of way, so it wasn't all bad. Just kidding. Funny story though. Last time I take a package from a shriveled granny without knowing what is inside—even if it was for her dying relative in Sarajevo! But it was a precious moment when the border guard handed my co-conspirator a butcher's knife to cut open the package. Trembling, she cut into the orange rind and the juice started to seep out. Oh, the adventures of the foreign correspondent. I wish. I was actually there on vacation, not corresponding about anything at all, just tagging along with a friend who was. I've been working in New York

since graduate school, covering fluffy stuff I'd just as soon not discuss. It's not as exciting as it was back in the USSR, babe, but I stay. It might be the golden handcuffs, but more likely it's because we have better coffee over here. Oh, the dangerous draw of complacency. Anyway, this story is my big chance to refresh my taste for the Moscow mix.

As far as the DC man—I still love him but can't be with him. He'll only convert if I convert and that won't really get us anywhere, now will it? It's a terribly long story, but the short of it is that, yes, I am still busily trying to find that nice Jewish doctor (or at least someone who can play one from time to time). Hopefully I'll find him soon, because the hunt is exhausting me (and probably my parents as well). Anyway, I will call you at home if that is all right, as I have a few things to attend to here. Some crazy rumor is circulating that Clinton had an affair with a White House intern and I need to make myself scarce so I don't get assigned to that tawdry tale.

Later, Jen

My timing was perfect. Just as I hit "send," Bill—the senior producer of the investigative unit—came out hunting for producers to send to D.C. Time to stalk the hairdressers and high school classmates. I jumped under my desk, cappuccino in hand, and sat there sipping until the story was safely assigned elsewhere.

When I emerged from the cover of my cubicle trench, I found the mail flag had sprung up again. I smiled and grabbed the mouse.

TO: jcohen@breakingstory.com
FROM: kdillard@spbpress.ru
DATE: January 20, 1998
RE: Re: re: re: whoring around the globe

Now it's a white house intern? And people ask me why I'm in Russia. Not that you can entirely escape that shit. Get this—last year, when Clinton et al were in town for the summit, a whore at the Grand Hotel National gave me a copy of Secretary of State Strobe Talbott's credit card receipt—$1,000 for room service! More specifically it was for her room service. And she claimed it wasn't just Talbott in the room.

Apparently, our tax dollars have been donated to insure those arrogant geeks get laid. Although, I haven't paid taxes in years, so I really don't care.

OK. Call me later. I need to finish throwing pencils at my staff.

K

Some girls are turned on by muscle, others by money. For me, journalistic prowess is a potent aphrodisiac. I grinned knowingly at my computer screen and wrote back again.

TO: kdillard@spbpress.ru
FROM: jcohen@breakingstory.com
DATE: January 20, 1998
RE: Re: Re: Re: Re: whoring around the globe
Dear Sir,
I am simply going to postpone judgment about the fact that you are romping around Russia cavorting with prostitutes. Glad to know you have some ins with that community as it will come in handy should you agree to help me out with this story. And you will agree to help me out with this story.

Will call in about two hours.

J

PS that you throw pencils at your staff I will judge immediately.

It's not like I decided then and there that I would actually pursue a romance with Kevin, but it was then and there, as I sent the e-mail off into the ether, that I felt that same pit-of-the-stomach swirl I had felt on the Charles River Bridge.

I reached for my cappuccino, thinking that it would focus me a bit, but I was down to that part when all that remains are the white crusty crystals of dried milk on the sides of the cup and a small, almost inaccessible ring of light brown liquid at the bottom. I made one last attempt to suck it all out before I stood up and marched toward Bill's office.

He was in rare form when I got there.

"I don't care what Krantz says. Find a fucking hotel room your-self. We are not going to miss this fucking story because you couldn't find a goddamn place to sleep in all of D.C.!" Bill was pacing in front of his phone—clearly on speaker—and waving a faxed copy of the tomorrow's *New York Post* cover: BILL SNARED IN SEX, LIES AND AUDIOTAPE.

He looked over the piles of papers on his desk and saw me lurk-ing in the threshold.

"Where the hell were you?" he said, motioning for me to enter the lair.

"I'm here, Bill," said the voice on the other end of the phone.

"No, not you. Just get your ass down there and call me when you hit the ground." Bill jammed his pointer finger into the disconnect button and directed his cross eyebrows in my direction.

"I was here, Bill. Working up a source for the trafficking story."

"I need you on this intern thing," he said, and visions of my pro-fessional life passed ominously before me. I could feel the coffee rid-ing up in my throat. Covering the president's intoxication with an intern while working at a tabloid would be the end of any journalis-tic credibility I might have. All the years of graduate school and dues paying would be wasted. I would never emerge from the sensational-ized trenches of tabloid TV. I had to save myself. I had to sell him the sex slaves. "This is a really hot story, Bill. The Russian story, I mean. Total sweeps story. I really think we should jump on it."

"We aren't *Dateline,* Jennifer. I don't have a staff of three hun-dred. I need you on this intern story. We can return to the sex-trafficking thing later."

"I hear *Primetime Live* is hot on it already," I lied. Well, it wasn't a complete lie. They were doing a story on sex-slave trafficking into Israel. Ours was better. I had been looking into a story about sex-slave trafficking into the United States, into Brooklyn. Word was, thousands of young women from the former Soviet Union were being lured here with promises of work as nannies and house clean-ers, only to have their passports confiscated by the Mafioso thugs who organized their transport. The women are told that without their passports, they don't exist. Then, terrified, they are forced to pay back their transportation costs and re-earn their identities by turning tricks in makeshift brothels or behind the stages of seedy strip joints. Any other time, this would have been the ultimate story for our syndicated television newsmagazine: tits and ass with a dash of respectable reporting. Toss in the international angle, and we could pretend for a few moments that we were the broadcast equivalents of Seymour Hersh.

"It's now or never, Bill. We need to jump on it," I said, walking up to his desk and pressing my hands flat on it.

He shook his head. "If Clinton was sleeping with these sex slaves, sure. But right now, that's the only way you are going to sell it to the EP." The EP is the executive producer of the show, the big boss.

"What if I could give you both sex slaves trafficked into Brooklyn and proof of Clinton administration officials using taxpayer dollars to party with Russian whores?"

Bill's ears perked up.

"Is there a connection here?"

"Just that both stories require my going to St. Petersburg."

"Can you prove those allegations about the Clinton officials?"

"My friend says if I go over there, he can show me a copy of the deputy secretary of state's credit card receipt for overindulgent room service."

"We don't have the budget." He started typing an e-mail message into his computer. Attention deficit disorder is practically a job requirement for anyone in television management.

"Plane fare in January is less than flying to L.A.," I said.

He hit send and sat down at his desk. "Go on."

2

Nᴇᴡ ʏᴏʀᴋ—When placing an international phone call to Russia, you have to endure an auditory attack of beeps and clicks before it is possible to actually begin speaking with your intended party. But when I called Kevin that evening, we had a brief moment of clarity before the cacophonous storm.

"Ia slushaiu," he said in Russian. It means "I'm listening." That's how most Russians answer the phone. Not "hello." Not "The Ivanov residence." Just *"Ia slushaiu,"* I'm listening. He wasn't the only one. Almost as soon as the connection registered, a battalion of bleeps and clanks and some odd whirring sounds came blaring across the line, drowning me out before I could respond.

"What the hell was all that?" I said as the noise finally retreated.

"Oh," he said, audibly dragging on a cigarette. "It's the FSB." The FSB is the successor to the KGB. Different in name but not in insolence. "Just ignore them. But if we get disconnected, wait a few minutes before calling back. They are sometimes slow about flipping the tape."

"You are totally shitting me," I said, tremendously impressed, mildly envious.

"No, I'm serious. Occupational hazard." Another sucking drag. A very audible exhale. "Wait! Fuck the FSB. Holy shit. It's you!"

"Hi." I giggled, schoolgirl-like. "How are you?"

"Good, good. God, it's nice to hear your voice." Again, an audible drag, another prolonged exhale. It reminded me of James Dean, and I blushed.

"How many years has it been?" Kevin asked.

"Well, I did leave a message on your answering about a year ago. Last time I was in Moscow."

"You did? I never got that message."

"It was sometime last January. I was there over New Year's."

"No shit."

Then there was silence, tension on the line. I was back in Boston, standing on the bridge. I carried the phone across my room and sat down on my bed.

"So, how is life in Russia?" I said, trying to think of something to say.

"Can't be beat. It's magical."

"Magical?"

"Black magic—but still."

"I should have stayed." I flopped over onto my stomach, approximating the pose of a teenage girl chatting on her princess phone.

"Not happy in New York?" he said.

"Not happy covering stories about the dangers of household appliances. There's not a lot of magic in it."

"What about your extracurricular life?"

"Not happy trying to date nice Jewish doctors," I said. "They aren't always all that nice."

"Try dating Russian women."

"Well, I'll bet they're not boring."

"They keep me on my toes."

"Toes getting tired?"

He said yes and joked that he could probably deal with getting some new shoes.

We laughed about our dating mishaps, about my inability to find someone who didn't bore me to distraction (or, if he didn't, who was willing to stick around), how I worried about my parents' worrying about my worrying about all this. Kevin complained about his string of empty affairs, said he wanted something more, that he functioned better when he had someone by his side but that the women he fell for tended to be married. He bemoaned the cultural disconnect that he sometimes felt, and I told him how envious I was that he had the strength to stay there, that he could make a life of that chaos. He told me, disconnects aside, that he couldn't imagine it any other way, that whenever he came stateside, he lost his way.

"There's no grip," he said. "Everything is the same from New York to Nevada."

"True," I said. "But if there were a Starbucks in Moscow, I'd be there in a New York minute."

He promised to inquire about their international franchise opportunities.

My company would probably not appreciate paying $2.50 a minute for this sort of banter but no matter. If asked, I'd say I was working up a source.

Kevin told me he wasn't all too sure he could find the Talbott receipt, but perhaps, after a thorough scouring of his office and maybe lifting his lumpy mattress at home, something would turn up. The trafficking story was a no-brainer, he said. He was already working on a similar investigation and had identified a variety of marriage brokers and travel agencies that fronted for the Mafia pimps and arranged for the visas. Shooting undercover video of these folks might pose some dangers, but it was within the realm of possibility.

That segment of the conversation took at most five minutes. For the better part of an hour, it sounded more like this:

"I always regretted that day."

"What day?"

"The day I didn't kiss you."

"What day was that?" I said, although I knew.

"It's funny we never did get together," he said, ignoring my question because he knew I knew.

"That would have required cheating, no?"

"I know. But there are worse things."

"Like what?" I knew what he was getting at, but I wanted to hear it. I wanted to know that the knotted-gut happy anxiety that I was starting to feel was something that he was feeling too.

"Like not knowing," he said after another long drag.

"I know," I said, smiling for him, even though he couldn't see me.

"Come here," he said.

"Find the receipt and I will."

Back at the office, the correspondent I'd been assigned to work with was as desperate to avoid Monica as I was to get to Russia, and between us we were able to sell the ideas. He and another producer focused on the domestic angle of the trafficking story—investigating strip joints and murders that had tenable links to New York's Russian Mafia. I pushed on the eastern end, speaking to Kevin many times a day to see what contacts he had made, what information he had dug up. And because I assured my boss that the Strobe Talbott receipt was in reach, he said he was cool with us pursuing the sex-slave story as well.

The swirling in my stomach morphed into a full body buzz. Professionally, I was on the path to my own sort of Pentagon Papers. And forget about nice Jewish doctors. At this point I wouldn't have been interested in one even if I were ill.

By the end of the week our phone bills were approaching thousands of dollars and my carpal tunnel syndrome had started acting up. We had prostitutes waiting to dish, pimps in the wings, Russian video crews on standby, and plane and hotel reservations being booked. Kevin still had not found the Talbott receipt, but by the end of the following week we were professing our love, discussing names for our children, talking about the books we would write, the trips we would take, and setting up job interviews in Moscow. I know it seems absurdly fast, but it was as if we had been channeling each other all these years, and now, now that we were actually communicating, I finally understood where all those prayers secretly spoken into pillows at bedtime had landed. No previous boyfriend got me so completely. Kevin said he had never been so completely gotten. The more we talked and whispered and plotted, the more everything—life—seemed to make sense.

In a college philosophy class we read Aristotle. He said something about love being a single soul inhabiting two bodies. I didn't feel exactly like that but close. It felt more like our souls were merged, overlapping over the phone lines. Like they shared our burdens, distributing the weight to a more manageable level. The thrill that gave me, the sense of lightlessness and ease, was intoxicating. And that intoxication gave me a sort of cocky spunk that infiltrated the rest of my life. It didn't last, of course, but it definitely existed. The e-mails we sent are like my own Gnostic Gospels (read those in a women's studies class)—written proof that once I really did feel that way.

TO: kdillard@spbpress.ru
FROM: jcohen@breakingstory.com
DATE: January 31, 1998
RE: The sweetest dreams cum true
    Hey there—
    I am bursting with adrenaline and would give just about anything for the opportunity to work it off rolling around in bed with you.
    But until then, here's the latest:
    I just scored an interview with a criminal informant for the CIA. She knows about everything we need to know. I think with a little butter she might introduce us to some very special characters. Meanwhile, my

boss is beginning to hem and haw about giving me a promotion (no, my darling, I have no plans for taking it—I am committed to coming to you) and a segment I did in December is being nominated for an award.

I am basking in this mildly arrogant sensation that my life is golden, and it's largely because of you. I can't imagine how wonderful it will be to actually be together.

I love you.

Jen

TO: jcohen@breakingstory.com
FROM: kdillard@spbpress.ru
DATE: January 31, 1998
RE: thief of my dreams
Hey, Sweetie—

I can't tell you how nice it feels to read what you wrote. I wish I could just go to bed now so I could dream about it, about making love to you in the middle of a fabulous cyclone. Which is what I did earlier, anyway. I can't wait for you to get your hands all over me. I can't wait to get my hands all over you. I am nearly in pain for want of you. How am I supposed to work in this condition?

I send you a deep, warm kiss between the folds of your lips.

K

I picked up the tickets.

Where did the concept of soul mate come from? If romantic love is just some sort of Victorian construct, then how can it be that this love thing so completely encompasses not only your mental but also your physical state? During the week leading up to my trip I was radiant. I was glowing like a pregnant woman, bouncing like a newborn. I grew about five inches. I swear. And my adult acne? My face bore no indication that I had ever suffered from it at all.

"I've never felt like this before," I said to my friend Erica. She was standing outside the D.C. hair salon where Linda Tripp got her dye job, and we were running up *Breaking Story*'s cell phone bill.

"Like what?" she said, but she knew what I meant. She changed the subject. "Can you believe what I am doing? It's practically too ridiculous to be embarrassing."

"You're not listening to me, Erica."

"I am listening to you, Jen. I've listened to you say this before. About Sam. About Dave. About Graham. About Matt. Am I forgetting anybody?"

"Point taken. But this is different."

"What's different? This time he's wearing the shining armor?"

"Seriously, it's different." I said, pleading. I wanted her to understand. This was a man who wasn't afraid to take the required leaps of faith, the ones I was never able to get anyone else to take with me. He had no fear. He chased Mafia dons and brought down mayors. He wasn't afraid to profess his love for me, sight unseen. And when he told me, sight unseen, that I was beautiful, that I gave him strength, I believed him. Our chosen paths, professional and romantic, were the same. "I have no doubt in my mind that he's the one, Erica. I'm serious. It feels different."

"Uh-huh. Tell me about it in a month."

"OK. Maybe outwardly it doesn't seem so different, but this time I know the guy."

"You haven't seen him in six years. Take a deep breath, Jen. You don't know him."

"I know him."

I did know him. How could you not know someone with whom you had been speaking for more than three hours a day for two solid weeks? I knew him. I knew all about his kinks and flaws. I knew all about his imperfections. I knew that his marriage failed because he drank himself into a detox clinic. I knew that he did more drugs in high school and college than Timothy Leary had in his whole lifetime. And I knew that he had founded the St. Petersburg branch of AA. His shit might have hit a fan or two, but so had mine. So has everyone's. Now we were both on track, and because we could be so honest with each other, because there was no fear or judgment between us, we were going to help each other stay there. In Russia, where we could love and work the way we wanted. It was so simple.

One night, as I lay tangled in phone cord on my bed, Kevin told me about Vicki. Right after college they moved to Berkeley and got married. Right after that they broke up. In the wake of it Kevin fled to live in Russia. But he could never really escape her. Vicki's name was etched into him, with thick gothic letters that wrapped around his left biceps, each one about an inch high. A leafy vine danced in the spaces between them and then wound around his skinny arm. Vicki was completely insane, he said. She was too much for him to bear. She took antidepressants like candy and spent a good four hours a week in therapy. There were whole months when she never left the house, and she hadn't held down a steady job since college.

I was silent and sweating as he told me this.

"What's wrong?" he asked when my nonresponse registered. "We can rework the tattoo to spell Jennifer. I know this great artist, and . . ."

It took a moment before I managed something.

"You know, I'm not exactly the most stable fish in this sea," I finally said.

"I realize that." He laughed. "So, how about we just cross a line through Vicki and write your name over it?"

"I've taken antidepressants before," I said.

"Oh. So? Which ones?"

"Well, I am on Prozac now."

I heard him inhale deeply. He didn't ask why I was taking it. At this point he knew enough about me that he didn't need to.

I nervously volunteered the information anyway.

"I went on it in college, to help with the eating disorder and stuff.

It worked really well, and I just can't find a good enough reason to go off," I said breathlessly.

"Doesn't it kill your sex drive?" He exhaled. "It devastated mine. I have to take Zoloft instead."

"You're on Zoloft?"

"Not now. But that's only because I can't find any in this city."

"Are you in therapy?"

He laughed again. "I'm in Russia."

"So who writes your prescription?"

"I pay Anastasia's father to do it."

Anastasia was an ex-lover who last year became pregnant with Andrei, and to this day it is unclear whether Andrei carries any of Kevin's DNA. But for harmony's sake, we just assume that Andrei is his father's son. Victor's, I mean. Anastasia's husband. Actually, there isn't anything shocking about this arrangement. Romantic lives in Russia make the characters in Milan Kundera's *The Unbearable Lightness of Being,* that saga of sexual musical chairs, seem tame. For example, one summer during my college years I was living in what was then Leningrad with my friend Vera, who was sleeping with her best friend Tanya's husband, Boris. Boris was also involved with Tanya's younger sister, Kyusha, but no matter. Vera was still involved with her ex-boyfriend Kiril, and Tanya was living with a guy named Efonya—who at one point made a pass at me. Meanwhile, Vera's father was involved with a French woman, who in turn left her German husband to become Vera's stepmother, and my Canadian boyfriend Peter had just married his ex-girlfriend Svetlana—ostensibly for a once-promised green card—so I started sleeping with my American friend Ben. No one was expected to comprehend these complications, but you were supposed to accept them.

"So this new information of mine is not threatening to you?" I asked Kevin when he finally focused on the subject at hand.

"Only if it kills your sex drive."

"But you just said that Vicki—"

"There are levels of nuts. Anyway, she's on lithium. Among other things. Really hardcore."

"Right. I know," I said, not really knowing.

"So, does it?" he said.

"Does what what?"

"Does the Prozac kill your sex drive?"

"No. At least not that I know of."

"Don't you think you would know?"

"One would hope."

"Seriously."

"That's all that matters to you, though?" I asked.

"That, and that it works for you, that you feel good."

Generally speaking, I find psychopharmaceutical discussions to be a bit like the *Lightness of Being* stuff. Sorting through the personal concerns about taking them and whether to be public about it is a bit like trying to waltz through a labyrinth when your partner has two left feet. I like to pretend it is a breezy thing, that I don't care what people think. But if someone is going to be my judge and jury, if he is concerned about these drugs' ability to change personalities and create false improvements—all I can say is he's wrong. I say that, even though a part of me also believes that he might be right. But the thing is, if someone can't understand the depth of hell that depression can drag a person to, or if he can't understand what it's like to have one's head in a toilet for about five years running, then he has no right to judge. If he cannot relate to my erstwhile ruminations of black sludge running through my veins and my fantasies of watching it all slowly ooze out of my arms, then sorry. He's just missing out. It is pretty interesting stuff, really. It's not about depression chic or easy answers. It's about so much more and about nothing at all. Sometimes it's just a vitamin I take.

I once had a guy literally jump out of bed when I told him I took meds. Not five minutes after he said he loved me. I've had other guys look at me with puppy-dog pity. And of course there has been loads of general dumbfoundedness. Kevin, however, had none of that. He got it.

It felt good.

"Can you get me some?" he wanted to know.

I laughed. "I thought you AA people were opposed to such tamperings."

"Live and let live."

"Such dedication," I said snidely.

"Don't." The word whipped out from him with such a snap that I hardly recognized it.

I changed the subject.

"I had a dream about you last night," I said, twisting the black curly cord around my fingers and closing my eyes.

"I dream about you every night." His voice was now soft, breathy.

I laughed again. "That goes without saying. But let me finish."

"Go on."

"In my dream you had no head."

"Really?"

"Well, you had a head, but it was a cartoon head."

"Go on."

"Actually, it was a cartoon heart. The way I imagine your tattoo, like a cartoon. Your head was an enlarged animated cartoon heart."

"That sounds about right."

"Which got me to thinking."

"Glad to help."

"I don't remember what you look like. I don't think I could pick you out of a crowd."

"I have an enlarged animated cartoon heart for a head," he said. "Hard to miss."

"Seriously. I don't remember what your face looks like. I remember you are skinny. Sorry, thin. You tend to be a bit unkempt. Tall, right?"

"Unkempt, tall, and skinny. That's me. And a cartoon heart for a head."

"I love you anyway."

"That's comforting."

"What do you picture when you picture me?"

"The most fabulous woman on Earth."

24

I couldn't help but smile. "Can you be more specific?"

"Sure. You are about five-four. Thin. Curvy. Big brown eyes. Brown hair. It was short when we graduated, but I imagine it long."

"It is long."

"Good. Not that it matters but good. And you have a beautiful nose."

"A large nose," I said. I wanted badly to accept his compliment, because, of all my attributes, nothing made me as self-conscious as my nose. "I look like Akhmatova," I said, referring to the famously angsty Russian poetess with the prominent beak.

"She had an exquisite nose."

"If you say so," I said, touching the bridge and actually liking it for a moment.

"I say so."

He said that he had a vivid memory of one night during college. He was standing on the second-floor landing that overlooks the student center, the place where we all milled about, flirting, drinking coffee, pretending to crack the books. Hundreds of people were there that night, he said. It was a zoo. But when he saw me (I was talking to some friends), it was like no one else was around.

3

S T. PETERSBURG — The plane begins its initial descent before the captain announces it, before the light goes "bing!" My blood is pumping so fast and furiously that the slightest lurch has become a serious threat to my inner balance. And my ears are popping. I do that forced yawning thing to stimulate my eustachian tubes as I powder my nose and reapply my lipstick for the tenth time.

"Would you like some more gum?" The missionary seems to pity me.

I take the gum and add it to the four pieces already in my mouth. Then the bing! sounds and the captain commands us to put our seats in an upright position. I close my eyes and try to take deep breaths, but it feels like the air is just not getting to the places it needs to go.

"Everything will be fine," says the missionary, "if that is God's will."

I don't believe in God, at least not in the sense of there being some old fellow with a long white beard who somehow has the time to watch and judge us all. If there is such a god, you would think he'd have better things to do than toy with my little life. But I do believe in karmic retribution, and I have done some bad things in my time. At Camp Emerson, for example, I gave a pair of Debbie Goldberg's period-stained panties to one of the boys' bunks (I wanted to impress Matt Levine). The boys in turn hoisted the panties atop a flagpole. In twelfth grade I wrote all the answers for my Russian final exam on my thighs. I cheated on my college boyfriend. Three times. And I have certainly sinned in my heart.

I don't take much comfort in this God's will thing, but, thank God, I do have faith in love.

The seat belt sign blinks off and we are free to move about the cabin.

I navigate my way from tarmac to transport bus, through the customs line, and over to the baggage claim. It's about ten o'clock in the morning local time, which makes it about 2 A.M. in New York. Or is it 3? I try to orient myself by looking for familiar signposts, but it has been more than seven years since that orgiastic summer when I last flew in and out of the St. Petersburg airport, so there really aren't any. I remember the bathroom as being on the right before the customs line and take small comfort that it is still there. Upon checking, I find that it is still free of toilet paper. This is the only continuity I can ascertain.

The last time I flew into St. Petersburg, it was called Leningrad. Gorbachev was president and there were lines for bread and ration coupons for sugar. You could still find quaintly crappy locally produced products, and cigarettes cost about ten cents a pack. Marlboros were a few kopecks more. And while I recall there being a few posters welcoming weary travelers and a dusting of low-key ads inviting them to consume, I certainly do not recall the blaring, almost neon, placards hawking nightclubs, casinos, and overpriced real estate that now clamor for airspace over the baggage claim carousel. They are glaring enough to shake me from my hyperadrenalized stupor. Not that I didn't expect them. That post-Soviet Russia is dramatically changing is common knowledge.

During the past few years Moscow has rapidly grown into a shoddy clone of Las Vegas. Every time I've been there (it's been seven or eight times since college—I've lost count), it seemed the casinos were reproducing. They spread like a virus onto virtually every corner of the city center. The lines of street prostitutes extend way beyond the midnight hours and into the next day's lunch. It seems as if McDonald's has provided a separate restaurant for every man, woman, and child, and you can't walk a block without tripping over a Coke bottle or a Snickers wrapper. But I had held out a hope that St. Petersburg's literary soul would somehow save it from the crass materialism that has infected Moscow. It didn't. The city does, however, maintain a bit of its old industrial flavor.

At least the air does.

The St. Petersburg airport smells like a gas oven that is slow to light.

I take some perfumed hand cream out of my carry-on and rub it into my palms before marching forward in search of a cartoon heart.

The missionary man disappears out the other side of the baggage claim, and once he passes, my view is no longer obstructed.

I see him.

I have had moments of satisfaction and pleasure in my life. Plenty of them. But no matter how happy or contented I may have been, never, not for one moment, have I ever felt the sensation of a solid click. But now, as I cross the threshold between the baggage claim and the waiting area, it happens.

My whole life just clicks into place. It is almost audible. I see Kevin and I hear the click.

I don't know whether to laugh or cry. I just know as I look at him standing there, tall and lanky, with a wide silly grin and an orange knit hunting cap holding down his outgrown crew cut. I look into his eyes, through his slightly fogged, round wire-rimmed glasses, and I know this is everything I have ever wanted.

There is a magnetic embrace. A passionate kiss.

And melting.

It isn't until we pile into the back of Sergei's red Lada (Sergei is Kevin's landlord and sometime chauffeur; his car takes a few minutes to get going) and breathe deeply a few times (not an easy task in the cold gaseous air) that I even realize that my soul mate has a face around his grin, under his glasses. A scraggy goatee that tickles my lips ("That's gotta go," I laugh). Tired but gentle eyes framed by a few premature crow's feet (from smiling). Teeth so stained and crooked that they could pass for European (how cosmopolitan). And a full, soft, grinning mouth that reaches out to kiss me again.

And again.

And again.

He envelops me in his tattered hard suede jacket. I breathe in the cigarettes and the years of Russian living that he is carrying around, its intoxicating weight. It is mysterious, thick with history and literature. And lust.

I inhale deeply, and so does he.

We've arrived home.

St. Petersburg, Russia, was built on a swamp and is precariously balanced on the bones of thousands of men. Built by edict and maintained by force, it is a beautifully cruel city, filled with cemented charm and a mystical grace. Everywhere you turn there are touches of evil decorated with hints of poetry.

A lot of poetry.

I pity the fools who think that Paris is the capital of romance. Because if romance is about passion and emotional extremes, there can't possibly be a more romantic city than St. Petersburg.

Fabulous facades battered down by the ages and the brutal winters mask crumbling interiors that house the warmth of families and lovers. Rivers and streams snake their way around the city streets, and in the winter the ice morphs the sidewalks into the embankment, creating a smooth, cunning, and continual field. In the summer the sun never sets, and in the winter it hardly shines but for the glimmer of a cupola over a church that reflects the midday attempt at light.

The Lada chugs down a narrow street and putters to a halt.

"That's my window," Kevin says, pointing to a balcony overlooking a snowy garden. It looks like the kind of balcony that Juliet might have stood on or from which Rapunzel would have let down her hair. "My fiefdom."

My prince.

Kevin lives in a building that once upon a time housed the servants of the tsars, the ones who did the laundry, to be precise. It's a castle. A dusty, graffitied castle of a matte grayish color that sits on a small island, across a rusty-railed bridge, in the middle of a canal.

We giggle and kiss and kiss again until we realize that Sergei has already begun dragging my stuff out of the car. We jump out to assist. Rather, Kevin jumps out to assist. I have crossed the Atlantic, which means that, as a woman, I no longer have to lift anything. Rape might be epidemic in Russia. Sexual harassment laws hardly exist. And wife battering is practically a given. But at least chivalry isn't dead.

I follow them through the threshold, down a dark passageway, out into the internal courtyard.

If you have ever read Dostoevsky's descriptions of St. Petersburg, you can imagine this scene. Kevin's courtyard looks just like the ones where Dostoevsky's characters once hung out. His building is like the home in which Raskolnikov, the main character from *Crime and Punishment,* tried to commit a perfect, untraceable crime. Lots of dirt and dark shadows. Crumbling walls and chipping paint. The air is infused with that magical misery. It's *tiazhelo,* as they say. It has weight.

After we pass under the clotheslines and over and around the discarded trash, we make our way into a stairwell that most certainly has some familiarity with Raskolnikov's murderous feet. The higher we climb, the less we can see. The wood stairs creak, and I am not sure they will hold me as I blindly step up toward Kevin's landing.

"I feel like someone might jump at me with a pickax," I say, and Kevin laughs. I laugh too, relieved that he got my Raskolnikov allusion.

No one does jump out at me with a pickax, of course, but as we walk into the tiny dusty foyer of Kevin's apartment, something lands on my head. Something with claws. It's a cat. A small dirty cat with rather sharp talons that are digging into my scalp. I try to shake him off, but he promptly crawls to the nape of my neck and starts sucking on my ear, tugging at my hoop earring with his teeth, whiskers scratching my chin. I giggle, because it tickles, but I can't shake him off.

Now the Dostoevsky reference is all wrong. Come to think of it, the whole scene is a bit closer to Bulgakov's surreal novel *The Master and Margarita,* in which a cat named Behemoth plays the devil's sidekick. That book takes place in Moscow, but we did read Bulgakov in that college seminar, and who doesn't love a full circle?

Kevin told me in an e-mail how he rescued the cat, then a kitten, off the cold city street, how he had nursed him to health, how they had become inseparable. Like Bonnie and Clyde, he said.

"So you tamed a wild beast," I say.

"Something like that." Gently, he peels Kesha off my ear.

"Stupid cat." Kevin rubs his nose against Kesha's like the cat is a baby or something. "He can't decide what color to be. Look." He holds Kesha up as if showing off a piece of jewelry, turning him to show the different sides.

It's true. Kesha is an odd blend of gray and beige but appears black at a certain angles. An anti-iridescence. He has both stripes and spots, long hairs and short. Some are even curly. Kevin tells me that because of a few traumatic early months on the streets of St. Petersburg, Kesha suffers from stunted growth in his hind legs and, all told, weighs about the same as a small loaf of black bread.

31

"This cat couldn't be anything but Russian," he says. "He's a mess, but isn't he beautiful?" He explains that the cat has an inner beauty, that Kesha is so confident that everyone will melt under his charms that everybody does.

Just like his daddy.

Sergei places the bags down and locks the door behind him on his way out.

"What a little Casanova," I say, scratching Kesha under his chin.

"He does the seduction for me. But I think this is where I step in," says Kevin.

4

ST. PETERSBURG—I wake up a few hours later and can hardly see. It is as dark as night, but it is three o'clock in the afternoon, at least according to the yellow Brezhnev-era clock that's perched on the bookshelf across the room and ticking so loudly I am convinced that it woke me up. It has two large metal bell domes on the top, not unlike those one might see in a Disney cartoon but very much unlike the silent quartz travel alarm that is buried in my carry-on. I really don't want to know what the Soviet alarm sounds like, so I throw off Kevin's polyester satin quilt and drag myself over, T-shirt in hand, in the hope of snuffing out the insufferable noise.

Before I reach it, the phone rings.

I let the machine pick up.

"Hey, honey. It's me. Are you there?"

Kevin.

I feel for the receiver.

"Hey," I say in a somnambulant whisper as I hold it to my ear.

"Hey." He could have said "tuna fish" and it would still have the effect of a Shakespearean sonnet.

"Hey," I say again, this time for real.

"Did I wake you?"

"No. Your clock did. But I had to get up anyway." I pause for a moment before addressing the awful truth. "We need to get to work."

"I know. But you looked so beautiful sleeping, I figured I would give you a few hours."

"Where are you?" It takes a moment for me to register that he isn't actually in the room with me. I have grown so accustomed to our electronic relationship that it seems natural to talk with a phone at my ear.

"Didn't you see the note?"

"I can't see anything."

"Oh. I thought I left a light on for you."

"I think the kitchen light is on, but it's pretty dark in here."

"You'll get used to that."

"Where are you?"

"I'm at the office. Leaving soon."

"Did you find the receipt?"

He laughs. "Let's talk about it in person."

I don't say anything for a moment.

"You OK?" he asks.

"You haven't found it?"

"We can talk about it later."

Shit, I think to myself. I don't say it aloud, though. I just say OK and turn the switch on the alarm clock to the off position.

We agree to meet at a nearby cafe. The only nearby cafe, actually. The Idiot, it is called, after another book by Dostoevsky, his commentary on the growing material crassness of nineteenth-century Russia. But first I have to leave word with New York and touch base with the local video crew that we hired. I need to shower and set up an interview with a woman who runs a marriage agency that allegedly fronts for one of these trafficking operations.

"Actually, do you mind setting up the interview?" I ask. "My Russian is rusty and I am too tired to deal with it."

"Your Russian is fine."

"You haven't even heard me speak it."

"But I know you're brilliant, and I am sure it is fine."

"Pozhaluista." Please, I say in exaggeratedly bad Russian.

"What do I get for it?"

"Aside from the two hundred a day we are paying you?"

"Aside from that."

"You know," I say, trying to sound sultry, "these bedposts are pretty sturdy."

"That works," he says, softly laughing. "I'll set it up."

"I'll see you in an hour," I say, opting to shower instead of work, instead of spitting half-truths into my boss's voice mail. No Talbott receipt and probably none coming. He won't be pleased. Best to just forget the rest and bathe in the glory of new love for the moment.

Literally.

A few years ago I was dating a guy named Joe. East Village Joe. Joe was one of those perpetually bohemian characters who show no signs of ever growing up. I liked him a lot. One of the things I liked best about him was that he had a bathtub in his kitchen. There was a grungy sweetness about having my morning coffee between shampoo and conditioner. I liked the collegial continuum his life offered, with stoned friends dropping by at all hours of the night and spontaneous road trips to IHOP.

Six weeks into the relationship, Joe broke up with me. It was completely out of the blue. And he did it at my office, no less. He had come by to meet me for a coffee break, but before I could even stir in the cream, he told me he was feeling stifled. He—on the eve of his thirty-first birthday—wasn't ready for the sort of serious "adult relationship" that he imagined I was looking for. He said the problem was something about my being everything he thought he wanted, but confronted with the reality of that, he wasn't so sure he was ready for it.

I was completely devastated.

But later that night, curled up on my living room couch, eyes dried out from hours of crying and a few too many episodes of *Frasier* and *Friends,* I had to admit, when pressed by my roommate, that I was more upset about some intangible idea of being rejected by Joe

35

the Perpetual Youth than about losing Joe the Guy. Joe had provided a salvation from the overly yuppified life in which I was so immersed despite myself. I was not a little bit overwhelmed with my rapid ascent (or was it descent?) into the trappings of adulthood. I was tethered to the practical constraints of a career path that seemed somehow to have chosen me. Instead of covering wars and shooting the deep documentaries that I had dreamed of, I was producing pretty but puffy packages that in turn produced the barely palpable but still respectable biweekly direct deposit to my bank account. Then, thanks in one part to the skyrocketing rents in New York and in another part to the small inheritance that fell in my lap when my grandfather died, I closed on an apartment on my twenty-fifth birthday. Adulthood does not start after your bat mitzvah. It starts when you take on a responsibility that you are not quite ready for. Joe took me away from that. Instead of calculating my mortgage rate or Christmas tips for the doormen, weighing Chinese takeout versus student loans or panic that with each late night ring of the phone another grandparent, aunt, or uncle, or worse—parent—had passed away or suffered a heart attack, instead of all that, I could finger the chipped enamel in his tub and pretend I was just another postcollege bohemian whose only worries were of the existential variety.

And now, as I walk into Kevin's kitchen and see a small rusty bathtub with a dripping faucet, as I watch the water slowly trace the long brown stain leading to the hair-encrusted drain, I smile.

5

S T. PETERSBURG —An hour later I climb back down the narrow staircase and, as Kevin instructed, follow the cracked sidewalk lining the bank of the Moika Canal. St. Petersburg is darker than I remember. A few streetlights keep me on course, but details are lost. With the absence of sight and my thick wool hat muffling sound, I feel a bit like I am tunneling through a dream. But I make my way toward the almost inconsequential bulb that Kevin told me to look for. It's dangling under an archway. I stand really close in order to read the tiny black letters painted across it. "The Idiot Café," it says. In English. I push open the heavy red door and go inside. A bouncer is sitting on a stool in the foyer. He grumbles something, but before I can ask what, he stands up and starts waving a handheld metal detector over and around me, like traffic cop or an overly enthusiastic priest. Nothing sounds, nothing beeps, so I'm allowed to descend through an unlit passage that leads to the main room.

Kevin is there, sitting alone at a corner table.

He sees me enter and his grin widens. As I approach him, I notice why.

He shaved off his goatee.

"Do you like it?" he asks, jutting out his hairless jaw.

I caress his smooth cheek and I kiss him. No answer could possibly be good enough, so I just kiss him again.

"So," I say, sitting back.

"So," he says.

"I guess you didn't find the receipt?" I take a sip of the lukewarm and watery cappuccino that he ordered before I arrived. "God, this is horrible."

"The cappuccino or that I can't find the receipt?"

"Both." I curl my lip and push the cup back to his side of the table. "Shit. You really can't find it?"

He takes a deep breath and picks up a cigarette that has been smoldering in the ashtray. After a long, exaggerated inhalation, he simply shakes his head no.

"Shit," I say again. My stomach lurches at the prospect of calling my boss and telling him the truth. This ill feeling is fleeting, however, a brief flickering of an instant, a *mig,* as the locals might say. I wonder, in this instant, if he ever had it, if the story was even true. I wonder if the truth is that it was just an exaggeration of an experience, a physical fantasy that he actually believed. But the truth is, I have had a slim, deeply suppressed suspicion all along that Kevin doesn't have and won't find the receipt.

So when I say, "You never really had it, did you?" it is not meant to be accusatory but rather conspiratory.

He protests. He insists he had it, insists it is a true story, and slowly shakes his head from side to side, looking baffled.

"I'm so sorry," he says.

It doesn't really matter, anyway. I'm here, aren't I? And isn't that the point? The other story, the trafficking story, is more interesting to both of us, anyway, but even that has really just become an excuse to be together.

"Whatever," I say, adding that without the receipt, we have no room for error in the trafficking story.

"No problem," he says and tells me that he has heard that we can find girls in the know at the Hotel National.

But the National is just a short walk away, and we still have a few hours, so Kevin grabs my hand to take me on a nostalgic tour up Nevsky Prospect, the Main Street of St. Petersburg. It was there, just off Nevsky, that I studied all those years before. I am curious to see how things have changed.

Back in the middle of the nineteenth century, Nikolai Gogol wrote about the bustling superficiality of Nevsky Prospect in his story, entitled, of all things, *Nevsky Prospect,* in which a talented artist falls in love with a tender ethereal beauty whom he passes on this street. It turns out that the young woman is a prostitute, and therefore in his mind she "ceases to be that weak, that beautiful being so different from us." And so the increasingly opium-addled artist decides to bring her to some sort of deliverance, so he can rescue her, return her to purity, and in turn she will, in some goddesslike fashion, rescue him. When offered this option, she laughs in his face. Dreams shattered, he kills himself. Of course the story is really about deception and projection, a kind of don't-read-a-book-by-its-cover morality tale, with this grand avenue as a central character. And it hasn't changed, the avenue. The beautiful details on the buildings, the sinewy statues on the bridges that cross the canals, these things could surely blind a person to the truth of this town, could certainly suggest a metropolis mindful of its manners, concerned about civility and sincerity—things that make a society work. You would never know at first glance that the hotels here still house whores, that behind the seams it's rather seedy. But isn't that the fun of things, the layers lent by stories told, the truth asking to be unmasked? And, as journalists, isn't that our job? So now, on an evening stroll at the end of the twentieth century, the other thing that comes to mind, literature-wise, and with special thanks to Mr. Williams and my eleventh grade advanced-placement English class, is *The Love Song of J. Alfred Prufrock.*

> Let us go then, you and I,
> When the evening is spread out against the sky
> Like a patient etherized upon a table
> Let us go and make our visit.

Everything is laid out for our amusement, a stage for us to perform pronouncements of affection for each other. It's like we have control over this mystical metropolis. Part of it, this feeling, is probably my jet-lagged confusion, part of it just ecstatic embrace, or rather the embrace of the ecstatic. The car exhaust smells like roses, and the hardened masses, moving like tattered-fur bumper cars down the sidewalks, appear to be doing a beautifully choreographed dance, one that we might have scripted. It is all so beautiful: the cupolas and the crowds, the snow banked against the curbs, and the dark sky that covers everything. I take a ton of flash photos, but the best picture taken isn't taken by me. A kerchiefed babushka catches my smile. She smiles back and I hand her the camera. We don't say anything as she snaps the shot. I am sure that it will look like it was taken by Robert Doisneau, that photographer whose work covers the walls of dorm rooms across America—the one with the French couple kissing in the street. He couldn't do any better.

I can picture it already, the photo: a tightly bundled couple is kissing in front of a dark bronze monument, which is illuminated by a few lights shining up from the ground. Catherine the Great. I think that is who it is. The snow sweeps all around and the ground is slick and frozen, but the warmth of the kiss melts the surrounding ice and invites a ray of sunshine upon the lovers. It's corny, I know. But I am sure that is how the photo will come out: with the otherworldly charm saturating our evening.

Even the idea that we are chasing pimps and whores as a form of courtship is kind of charming to me.

Right.

Prostitution, sex slaves. That was why we are here. That and the fucked Strobe Talbott receipt.

We meet up with the crew back at Kevin's and then head off to the bar at the Hotel National to chat up some girls.

The crew—two English-speaking guys from a local St. Petersburg television station—wait in the car outside as we walk through the glass-enclosed metal detector and past the large men in dark Italian suits. The bar is fairly empty except for three clusters of sultry, long-legged women and one cluster of boisterous, drunk British businessmen. We settle into a small table near a female cluster, and Kevin orders two mineral waters and a pack of Marlboro Lights.

He offers a cigarette and I take one. He lights it for me and we smile. And once we work out a good line of questioning, he goes over to talk to the whores.

You have to admit it: There is an undeniable sexiness to covering the sex trade. It's like covering wars. And there's not much that is sexier than that.

"What did they say?" I ask rapid-tongued when Kevin returns to our table.

"They are worried that you're taking their business."

"What?"

He says the British businessmen were leering at me and they thought . . .

"Oh, Christ. You set them straight, right?"

"Yeah. I said you only whored yourself in the name of television news."

"Ha, ha. Very funny."

"Seriously, though, I told them you're my bitch."

"That's so sweet," I say sarcastically but sort of liking the implication that I am his. We are each other's.

He lights another cigarette and leans forward.

"They also said there's a girl at Dolls who just returned from working in Israel, and she might know a thing or two."

I pull him toward me and kiss him.

Dolls is located just up Nevsky from the National. But it's freezing outside, so I ask Nikolai, the cameraman-cum-chauffeur, to drive us up.

"You can be our getaway car," I say and tell him to park in front of the club.

Kevin walks ahead of me, and I have to jog to catch him at the club's door.

"Wait," I say.

"What?"

"What's our plan?"

"Just follow me."

I do. Walk in. We check our coats.

There is, right after the coat check, a very large, very black man sitting on a stool. "Five hundred rubles," he says in English. I can't place his accent.

"For her too?" Kevin says, touching my arm.

"Especially for her."

We don't have five hundred rubles. We don't even have fifty. "Where are you from?" I ask, lifting my chest ever so slightly, offering a coquettish smile.

"Why you care?"

"I like your accent."

"Nigeria," he says. "Six hundred rubles." At the present exchange rate that's about $40.

I raise my eyebrows.

"I joke," says Nigeria. "Six hundred for both."

"Do you take American Express?" I ask, fishing for my corporate card.

"Visa," he says.

"See," Kevin whispers in my ear, "it's not so difficult to run up a credit card bill on whores around here."

"You don't need to prove the Talbott thing to me."

"I know."

"But imagine what this is going to look like on my expense report."

After running the card, Nigeria lets us pass.

Why is it that whenever you enter a seedy underbelly type of place, it always seems familiar? It's like they are all modeled after the same Hollywood image of what they are supposed to be, so there they are. Art creates life creates art. And on and on. Dark room, hard seats. Men, looking more bored than turned on, slouching in the seats, watching. A pulsing strobe makes the dancing girls, the ones swinging around the pole and collecting cash in their G-strings, seem a bit robotic.

We sit down at a small cocktail table far from the stage. A waitress brings us the cola we ask for and Kevin starts to smoke.

Here's what happens. Two topless blond girls pull up chairs and join us for conversation. Natasha and Natasha. They are really nice, actually. And, oddly, it doesn't feel sexual at all. They ask where we are from and we say that we are tourists from New York. They compliment my Russian, they comment on how cute we are.

"*Kak tebe povezlo,*"—you're so lucky—says Natasha Number One, the one with, I think, her own breasts. She whispers in my ear that Kevin is adorable, so sexy how he smokes his cigarette, and so clearly in love, the way he keeps looking at me. She says she once had a boyfriend who looked just like him. Small round glasses, overgrown disheveled hair. He was a fabulous lover, she says and sighs. I tell her that Kevin and I haven't actually had sex yet. Not quite. At least I think that is what I say. My Russian is very rusty.

It will be great, she tells me, and I tell her that I know.

We are like girlfriends, giggling and trading little secrets, me and the whore.

Kevin, meanwhile, is deeply engaged in a conversation with Natasha Two. Of the fake breasts. They don't move, even when she nods, animated, and leans over to whisper something in my Natasha's ear. I look at Kevin quizzically. He smiles and gives a subtle thumbs up.

"Two hundred dollars," Natasha One says to me. In English.

"What?" I look at Kevin.

"They know things," he says through his teeth. He says they can come back to his place with us. To talk. Even on camera.

"We can't pay for an interview."

"We can pay for their time," he says. "They are on the clock."

I think about this for a moment. "Let's just take one."

And so it goes that for one hundred dollars my Natasha, clad in an absolutely enormous fur coat, tottering in her stiletto heels, follows me and Kevin out of the club. Nigeria gives me a pat on the ass when I walk past him. It feels somehow OK, validating.

And so here I am, sitting in the back of a crappy old car, sandwiched between my smoky soul mate on one side and a thickly perfumed, very well-insulated prostitute on the other. She is pretty, actually. Very pretty. She emits that kind of feminine mystique that I can never seem to capture for myself. Her makeup is flawless. Her hair is luminous, like spun gold. I want to touch the strand that has fallen out of the large black clip holding the rest of it off her neck. Her nose is perfect, straight and small. I touch mine. It's not that. I wonder whether Kevin finds her attractive. I wonder whether he is disappointed with me, now that he sees me after six years. He has been surrounded by beautiful Russian women. He can have his pick of them. He's an American man who earns dollars and has a valid passport. And she thinks that he is sexy.

Natasha feels for the unruly strand and undoes the clip. She shakes her locks loose, like a character in a shampoo commercial. In fact, I can smell it, the shampoo. I look at Kevin. He's staring out the car window, thank God. But he must feel me staring at him, because he turns around.

"What's up?" he says. He runs a gloved finger over my cheek.

"Nothing." I put my head on his shoulder and no one says anything as we drive up to his building.

We are back in Kevin's apartment, and the crew is setting up the camera and lights. Nikolai flicks on the Tungsten, illuminating Natasha's face.

She is drawn, tired. Slouching in a chair set up opposite me. Suddenly, she is different. Enough makeup to cover a clown. Pushing forty, maybe. Not the under-thirty I had taken her for. She inhales a cigarette, and I notice that her bright red lipstick is feathering out into the creases that circle her mouth.

"Pull the light back a bit," I tell Nikolai.

He does.

"Let me see the monitor." The monitor is on the floor, at my foot, but it's facing the wrong way. Nikolai turns it toward me and switches it on. Natasha asks to see it too, and when she does, she insists that she told me that she had to be silhouetted.

"They will kill me, you know." She says this in a very matter-of-fact manner. Like, "pass the salt, please" or "nice day we are having."

"Of course," I say, as if I know. Wanting to know but not asking: If her life is so tenuous, is it more or less precious? Does she take more or less pleasure in spring buds and the sun's rays? If you cheapen your body, do you strengthen your soul? Is there any relief in knowing that someone else controls your fate?

We rearrange the lights. Now all you can see in the monitor is a big dark blob with a halo.

"Natasha, can you sit up a bit?" I tell her. "Kevin, you'll sit here, next to me, but I want her to look at me, not you. Not the camera. No, no, Nikolai, that angle is too wide. Push in. Right. OK. Can you soften that light a bit more? Still. It's not right. Pull it back. She looks like she is a fucking alien." I am a producer. A professional. I am ordering them all about, willy-nilly.

Kevin is grinning.

"What?"

"Nothing. You're just kind of sexy being a bitch."

"I am not being a bitch."

He kisses my cheek. "It's cute."

I roll my eyes, but the truth is I like that he said that. "Can you get Natasha something to wear?" Natasha is still wearing her fur, and I am not sure that she has anything under it.

Kevin hands her a washed-out, once-blue Oxford shirt. Nikolai adjusts the lens. Sasha, his sound tech, walks over to run the lavalier microphone up her shirt.

"I can do that," I say and take it away from him.

Natasha acts like she doesn't notice that I am dragging a mic cord against her bare chest, across her skin.

45

I am touching a prostitute's breast.

She keeps on smoking, paying me no mind. I clip the lav to her collar and sit back down.

"Some people would pay good money to do that," Kevin whispers to me.

"We are paying good money," I whisper back.

"Rolling," says Nikolai, once the lens is properly focused.

When I was in graduate school, one of my professors, an old-time newspaperman, lamented my decision to pursue a career in television news. "Another loss for print journalism," he wrote on my review. In person, he pressed me on my decision, and all I could really say was that I enjoyed working with visuals. But the truth about working with visuals, as with all forms of voyeurism, is that it's not just about the pretty pictures. It's power. Remember all that film theory that equates the camera lens with the phallus, photography with some sort of rape? It might seem like good fodder for college coffee-shop chats, but the vulnerable really do lie on the other side of the lens. Toss into the equation network news call letters or the name of a popular program, and people quake at your request. Sometimes I think that we, the producers calling the shots, are like modern-day Napoleons, making up for our personal inadequacies by the use of an almost insurmountable force. From this angle we control things.

"Natasha," I say, "tell me how you became a prostitute."

She sits up straight, as if she were under interrogation, and she tells us (well, she tells Kevin because I have him translate my questions, just to be sure I am getting the right point across) that she entered this profession just because she likes it, because the money is good, and, as a girl from the provinces, she was drawn to the glamour that the money and the men provide. She says that she is a career woman like any other.

"The only difference is where the money comes from," she says, looking at me and then nodding toward Kevin. At least my parents are proud of what I do for a living, I think, and, with a defensive giggle, I get back to the subject at hand.

"How can you like it?" I ask. "You are completely giving up control over your own body. Isn't that frightening?"

She glares at me like I am a little kid asking an incredibly naive question.

"Look at those men drooling over the girls in the club," she says, "and then tell me who has the control."

But what about the pimps who take part of their money? what about trafficking? what about the women who have been forced into this profession? I ask her.

She says that she does know of women who were kind of forced into the trade, especially after traveling abroad. Or when traveling abroad.

"They are idiots if that surprised them," she says. "I mean, everyone knows about those scams."

I ask what she means, why she should assume the women are all idiots.

"Oh, come on. What do they think? That life is a fairy tale and with the rub of a golden fish all their dreams will come true?" She went on about how too many people just assume that they deserve good things, that they think that they shouldn't have to really work or try too hard. It's a pretty typical complaint that you hear in Russia these days, that people are so used to waiting for government handouts and subsidies that they have no work ethic. They say this about Russia, but I don't think that we are all that different. Doesn't everyone dream of the quick fix, the lotto win, instant fame, love at first sight, and happy endings?

I ask her to tell me about these women, the idiots.

"My own sister was in Germany for a year," she says. "She thought that she was going to be a babysitter. What a fool. Anyway, she's back now. Turns out she likes the work too. She's at Luna. We can go meet her later if you want."

"*Da, da,*" I say, not waiting for Kevin to translate. "*My ochen' khotim vstretit' ee.*" We would very much like to meet her.

I quickly wrap the interview, telling the crew to leave the light stands in place, hurrying everyone out of borrowed shirts and through the door.

We spend the next five hours rushing like this. Until daybreak. Finding women who have worked abroad, pulling them into snowy back alleys for "anonymous" interviews. Some demand a little cash for their time, others don't. Ethically, I suppose that it is a bit suspect to pay someone you are interviewing, but given the circumstances and given that I can in no way come home empty-handed, we justify it, especially when a pimp comes at us from around a corner.

He is large. That is really all I notice when he lunges at Nikolai. He is really, really big.

I don't understand what he is saying. Lots of curses and stuff. Not language I learned in school.

Sasha somehow grabs the camera from Nikolai's shoulder and runs with it to the safety of the car. Like it's a football play or something. Nikolai falls on the ground, and Kevin is cursing back at the pimp. His street Russian is flawless. They start doing that shoulder-push bravado thing that guys do, like in a bar fight. "Stop it!" I am yelling, and I find myself digging into my pocket for the remaining dollars. I tell Kevin to give them to him. The money. To give it to the pimp. He just keeps cursing, and they keep pushing at each other's shoulders. This guy is about twice as wide as Kevin. Substantially taller. The woman, meanwhile, has disappeared back into the club. Nikolai stands up and steps in, but he is smaller than Kevin, and I am screaming that they should just give him the money that I have in my hand. But the pimp is demanding the tape from the camera. He doesn't seem to care that I am trying to push the money at him. Which I now am. Reaching up with a wad of cash, waving it at him. He slaps my arm away and the bills tumble to the ground. There must be about two hundred dollars. We are all distracted by this, the fluttering of the bills, and Kevin grabs me. We, with Nikolai, dash into the car and drive away, the pimp screaming at us, disappearing in size and sound as we speed down the street.

I once saw a show on the Learning Channel about how what you do on a first date very much affects the beginning of a relationship.

They strapped all sorts of heart-rate monitors and electronic things to the "singles" and discovered that novelty, adventure, and surprise were much more effective aphrodisiacs than candlelight and wine.

Which brings me back to the polyester satin quilt.

Sex is destined to be at least a little steamy after a month of phone foreplay and cyberseductions, but add to the mix an evening with prostitutes and pimps, and you are pretty much guaranteed a wild ride. Toss in the whole being-in-love thing and it will blow your top.

"I am so madly and completely and insanely in love with you," Kevin says when we are finally back at his place and warming up in bed.

"I want to be together when we die," I say.

"We will be."

We plot out the books that we will write and the films we will shoot. The stories we will break and the careers we will create. We talk about getting married, and we laugh at how we will strap our infant children on our backs as we catch the next train to the latest war zone.

"Kosovo's going to blow," I say.

"Spring break in Kosovo," he responds.

We caress each other from mouth to toe, tangling with the fantasies that we have been building up, savoring each kiss while eagerly anticipating the next.

I trail my fingers along the line of his ribs, which stick out like a Braille path, leading me I am not sure to where, but I am eager to find out. He is even skinnier than I imagined, stomach caved in, hip bones jutting out. I kiss them, his hipbones, tracing their feminine curve with the tip of my tongue, loving how unique and wonderful this all feels.

Kevin moves down, gently pressing his lips across my inner thigh. Instead of tensing as I normally might, I relax into this moment and feel my legs go slack.

Fingers intertwined, breath heavy, we move together until we are finally indulging ourselves in a few moments of a warm and glorious silence.

"I love you," he says, breaking the spell, casting another one.

I kiss him and we begin again.

After a while, after a few cigarettes and a few more satisfied kisses, we banter a little and then I roll tight into the smooth but ratty comforter, offering my back to be spooned.

"Thank you," he says.

"For what?"

"For sending me that first e-mail."

I laugh. "Glad I'm here, are you?"

He tells me that with me next to him, he feels a bit like he is escaping his life, like he is being released. I say that I know what he means, pull his arms tight around me, and start to close my eyes.

"I like divorce," he says as he nuzzles into the nape of my neck.

"What?" I say, eyes open, more confused that he wants to keep talking than by the line itself. Until it registers. "What?" I say again, this time turning back to face him.

"It's a line from a poem. It's fucking brilliant. Listen." He turns over and picks a magazine up off the floor, its pages already open, yellowed.

"What is that?" I say, not wanting to listen and blindly try to grab the magazine out of his hands.

"Last month's *Harper's*. Listen."

"How the hell did you get *Harper's* here, of all places?"

"My mom sent it." He pulls it farther out of my reach and into the chill of the room, too far from the warmth of the sheets for me to venture toward it. "Listen."

I retract deep into the bed and shut up.

"'I like divorce,'" he begins again.

"That's a really nice start," I say from under the blanket.

He continues:

> I like divorce. I love to compose
> letters of resignation; now and then
> I send one in and leave in a lemon-
> hued Huff or a Snit with four on the floor.

Do you like the scent of a hollyhock?
To each his own. I love a burning bridge.

Kevin finishes reading the poem and, after an approving cluck of his tongue, passes the magazine over to me.

"Wow," I say, grabbing it. "That is so perfect!"

"I love the smell of a burning bridge," he says, laughing as he misquotes a line from the poem.

I smile and roll over to kiss him. "We can roast marshmallows over the flames."

IN THE SKY—Two days later we are sitting in the back row of an Aeroflot flight to Moscow, preparing for interviews at the U.S. embassy and the Russian Ministry of the Interior. We are settling back into the threadbare seats, noting the improvements in the in-flight service. Kevin says that he once had to share a seat with a goat, and I tell him about the time I saw a dog piss in the aisle. But there are no noxious animal smells in 1998. Just human ones.

We are sandwiched between an oversized Chechnyan man who apparently does not believe in personal hygiene and a New Russian woman who seems to believe that showers are best when Chanel No. 5 is substituted for water.

I burrow my nose into the creases of Kevin's neck.

"I can't believe I am really thinking about living in this country," I say into his smoky skin.

"Oh, but you are."

"I am."

"So we move to Moscow and then what?" he says, continuing a conversation that we have been having for weeks now. We already have agreed that we both need to be in Moscow. It is an ugly city, but it is where the news bureaus are. It is the only place we can both push our careers forward.

"Well, I score my dream job as a network news producer and you win a Pulitzer Prize for the *New York Times*." I say this very matter-of-factly, as if it is a given.

"I see."

"It's not so far-fetched."

"And if I don't get a job at the *Times*?"

"You'll get a job at a different paper."

It really isn't so far-fetched. During the past year Kevin has been contacted by the *Independent, New York Newsday,* and the Associated Press. And as far as my own employment is concerned—well, I've had problems sticking with jobs, but scoring them is another matter. I already have interviews lined up with the Moscow bureaus of CNN, NBC, and WTN.

"You sure you want to do this?" he says.

"Move to Moscow with you? More than anything in the world. Are you sure you want to?"

He just kisses me and smiles.

"So," he says, "where will we live?"

"We have to live in the center. I am not doing that bus to trolley to metro thing every day."

"Rents are out of control in Moscow."

"We will be rolling on the back of the mighty tax-free American dollar," I say. "We can live anywhere."

"How about one of those Stalin skyscrapers?"

"Totally. Maybe we can have Beria's old pad."

"Or boot out Pugacheva."

"Neighbor Berezovksy."

"I think he lives in the 'burbs."

"Oh, wait," I say. "I just remembered something."

"What?"

I pull myself a bit away from him and give a conspiratorial shrug. "I once made a promise to myself that I would never live with a guy unless I was at least engaged to him." I am only half-jesting. We have already plotted out our children's naming ceremonies and our grand-children's birthday parties. There is little question that we will be married; it is just a question of when.

"OK." He smiles wider and he pulls me closer. "Will you marry me?"

The jesting stops. Knowing, assuming, wanting—those are fine and well. But hearing—actually hearing—the words I have dreamed of since I was, I don't know, maybe five, it shakes me.

I start to cry.

"Really?" I say.

"Really, what?" he says. "Do I want to marry you?"

"Yes."

"Yes," he says and cradles my cheeks in his palms as he kisses me. "I want to grow old with you and love you and be everything to you." I can smell the stale cigarettes as he breathes out the words again. "Will you marry me?"

I wipe some tears with the back of my wrist, smile, and sputter a yes. Then I furrow my brows and whisper in a tone that I must con-fess is not unlike baby talk. "I want a ring," I say, pouting.

Kevin holds up his bony hands. They are adorned with chunky silver on almost every finger. "One of these will have to do for now."

He has a puzzle ring. It is made of two stick figures—a man and a woman. Basically, when the puzzle is put together, they're fucking. He takes the woman and I take the man. Kevin slides it into place.

"It's beautiful." I laugh and we kiss again. I hold up my hand to examine the ring. "God, look at the dick on this guy. In human pro-portions it would be about two feet long."

"A twenty-four-karat dick," he says.

So it isn't a reenactment of my age-old fantasy that includes kneel-ing, roses, and a huge diamond—perhaps some champagne and caviar—but it is good enough for a little while. I feel more complete than I have ever felt in my entire life. I am engaged. It is the perfect state to be in. Full of potential and celebration. Full of attention and adoration. I want to be engaged forever.

"*My zhenimsia.*" We're getting married, I say to the flight attendant who is handing out piping-hot coffee in thin paper cups. She doesn't say anything, but I don't care. I take the coffee—instant and watery—and we begin our descent.

7

Moscow—The year has only begun, but anyone can tell you that 1998 is going to be a pivotal one for Russia. The winds of change are already blowing strong when our plane hits the cracked tarmac at Moscow's Sheremetevo Airport. They blow far beyond the fumes leaking from the carrier engines and the slushy potholed ground that we skip across on our way to the terminal-bound transport bus. There is plenty of reason to be concerned and, for an aspiring foreign correspondent (like me), to be excited. Boris Yeltsin, citing the nagging effects of a lingering viral infection, has just taken off on a sudden vacation. "The Asian flu" is ransacking the economies of Indonesia and its neighboring states, and the ruble is struggling to fight off infection. Foreign Minister Yevgeny Primakov is busy cutting deals with the Iraqis for one nuclear power plant or another. Local reactors are leaking, Mafia gangs are killing, incurable diseases are spreading, soldiers are defecting, and unpaid workers are protesting. The list is long and the ink is wet. One strong gush and all the text will bleed together into an indecipherable mess.

We unload from the transport bus, and Kevin desperately lights up a cigarette. As he inhales, I exhale.

"Aren't you afraid to light up in this air?" I say.

He laughs and grunts a mock combustion sound. I laugh and grab his arm. We push our way through the gate, and my old friend Elena is there to greet us as we emerge from the crowd. A smile spreads across her round, doll-like Slavic face when she sees us.

"When are you two moving to town?" she says in Russian, before I even have a chance to introduce them. But Elena is the kind of friend with whom you can pick up a conversation after a year of silence and not miss a beat.

Our friendship goes back to that Kundera summer of love swaps and sob stories, the summer when Yeltsin climbed on the tank and the Soviet Union began to unravel. Elena is a university friend of my friend Vera's—Vera who was sleeping with her friend Tanya's husband, Boris, and so forth. A few years before that, Elena fell in love with a doe-eyed boy named Mikhail, who was, quite literally, a prince. She moved to Moscow to be with him. When things got really nuts up in what was then Leningrad, Vera and the gang, my gang, leaped on an overnight escape train and joined Elena and Mikhail in their Moscow pad. I went with them.

Mikhail inherited the apartment at Rechnoi Vokzal, the final stop on the metro's Green Line, when he was eighteen. It was then, in the mid-1980s, when glasnost was opening a few more doors, that the last holdouts on the maternal side of his aristocratic family decided to give up on the Motherland and jump at the chance to emigrate. Mikhail jumped at the chance to be the only one in his crowd with his own apartment. It was a great apartment by any standard, not just in comparison with the cement Soviet slabs that surrounded it or the crumbling building that it was holed up in. Two cavernous rooms absorbed heated blankets of sun through the wall-sized windows that enclosed them. The wood-paneled floors were worn to the perfection sought by Manhattan's most coveted interior decorators. Over the rusted railings on the thin balcony, you could look out over a forest lush enough to mask the hustle and hell of the street market directly below.

In the years after college, I repeatedly flew across the ocean to do nothing more than hang out there. It became my resting place and restorative spa. I have even gone to visit in the dead of winter—a time most of my peers were heading to the Caribbean or Mexico to relieve their rat-race–related stress. While they were soaking up ultraviolet rays and tossing back gin and tonics, my Russian friends and I were sitting around on unstable furniture (the broken Soviet television set was our table, old milk crates our chairs), drinking tea (and vodka), smoking cigarettes (and hash), and talking about anything that came to mind (and nothing at all). People stopped by and stayed the night. Some stayed longer. There were never enough beds, but it never seemed to matter. And through the years, from the venue on *Festivalnaia Ulitsa* (Festival Street), I watched my generation of Russians grow up. Through the years I guess they also watched me.

Now Elena and I are leading Kevin up the disintegrating steps into the building, past the graffiti scratched on the green corridor wall, up the nine flights of stairs (placing our jacket sleeves in front of our faces to mask the urine scent in the cramped elevator), and into the apartment. In the years between my visits a crib has replaced the tattered couch and a real spring mattress has arrived in the bedroom. Elena and Mikhail had gotten married under an onion-domed cupola, and most of their friends have learned to call before dropping by. Mikhail is designing decent but consuming career-building websites and computer programs, Elena is studying to be an architect, and three-year-old Dimitri (Dima) is starting preschool in a few weeks.

We throw down our bags and collapse around the new kitchen table. Mikhail turns off the thirteen-inch Sony color television (factory stickers still on the corner of the screen) and sits down to join us.

"Privet." Hi. He nods and stretches to grab a pack of Parliaments lying at the far end of the wooden table. Before he can tap a cigarette out of the pack, Kevin intercepts and hands him one of his own L&Ms.

"Spasibo." Thanks, Mikhail says, and smiles ever so slightly.

Kevin smiles back. *"Pozhaluista."* Please. No problem.

Elena and I shoot satisfied glances at each other.

We spend about an hour sitting there as Kevin regales us with stories of Elena's native St. Petersburg. She and Mikhail pepper him with questions, and Kevin tells them all about the recent McDonald's bombing and Mafia hits, the phone taps and the funeral wreaths. I listen to his almost unaccented Russian (with an occasional English aside, for my benefit), his flawless storytelling skills (at appropriate pauses he touches my leg or the back of my hand), the way he can build a simple plot to a crescendo and crack a joke at the absolute perfect point.

The L&Ms are polished off and we start in on the Parliaments.

"Since when do you smoke?" asks Elena as I gesture for Kevin to light me up.

"I figure it's better to breath your Moscow air through a filter," I say, laughing at my stilted Russian. Kevin swings his arm around my shoulders and kisses me hard on the cheek. Elena laughs too and lights up.

"A toast!" says Mikhail. He takes a final deep drag, snubs out the butt, and stands up. "I'll be right back." He laces up his boots and tosses on his thick down coat, not buttoning it as he bolts out the door.

"Isn't he going to freeze out there?" I say.

"He's used to it," says Elena.

Five minutes later Mikhail blows back in, spreading the frozen air that he has carried from the kiosks as he whips a bottle of vodka from behind his back.

I look at Kevin. He appears unfazed. When the vodka starts flowing, he declines so gracefully that I doubt Elena or Mikhail even notices. "I've gotten good at this," he whispers in my ear.

I gently nod, approvingly, because in my experience the stereotypes are true: In Russia vodka is lifeblood, and for a man to decline a drink is more often than not a sure sign that he is a sissy, sick, or just plain pathetic. For Kevin to be able to hold his hand over the shot glass and not join in the bacchanalia (and to decline to do so with such confidence and grace) is the most profound sign of maturity, bravery, and glory that I have ever encountered. For him to be so willing to explain the rejection is beyond the pale.

"You sure?" asks Mikhail, holding the bottle in a position prone to pour.

"Yeah. I don't drink," Kevin explains. "I'm an alcoholic."

I suppose that it is not for me to describe that fragile fight against the beast of addiction. But I have been around and through enough self-inflicted torment to at least understand the heroism required. I understand what it takes to break free of the impulse to sabotage yourself, the compulsion to jump into a spiraling vortex of despair.

At least I like to think that I understand it.

I admire his tenacity and grace right now. His ability to stay clean in this country makes me feel somehow protected, like it's proof positive that he can part waters for me, if need be, that he will stand straight where other lovers' spines have curved. But quietly, I also wonder whether we will ever share a full-bodied bottle of Chianti over a pasta dinner or if he will be able to drink to the toasts at our wedding. Maybe these are attainable goals if aided by a touch of will and power. Maybe, on some level, this romance with alcoholism is nothing more than an accessory to his artistic vision of writer, world traveler, dream lover. Maybe we can sip together.

"We should get going," I say and kiss him with my vodka-stained lips.

"Right," he says. We excuse ourselves and go to the bedroom to change.

8

Moscow—St. Petersburg gave our investigation a juicy share of leads, but the juiciest of all comes not from a pimp or a whore or even from St. Petersburg. It comes from an old friend of Kevin's. Kevin told me that his friend was an ambitious American journalist whose deadly combination of arrogance and brilliance had gotten him fired from a fair share of Western media outlets. Given his record, this friend could do what he did only in Moscow, a city without copyright or libel laws worthy of the names and plenty of willing investors hungry to back any venture: He started his own newspaper. Like any business in town, the paper has a *krysha,* a "roof" of Mafia-backed protection. It just so happens that the paper shares its *krysha* with one of the most scandalous casinos in town, the Beverly Hills. Through that connection Kevin's friend got wind of a dancer named Olga, who had a friend who recently escaped from a stint at sexual servitude in a Brooklyn cellar and who might be willing to talk.

I zip up my tall black boots and straighten out my short black skirt, the one with buttons down the front, trying to monitor my reflection in Elena's tarnished bedroom mirror. I'm trying to look fearless.

"What do you think? Good camouflage?" I say, hands on my hips. Kevin says that I make a glamorous *shpion-chik,* a spy girl. I laugh and relax the pose.

"And the hidden camera goes where?" he asks, tucking in the last corner of an overstarched white shirt that has clearly been victimized by Soviet-strength dry cleaning.

"Right here." I lift my skirt. The small camera is strapped to my right inner thigh and the lens pokes through a buttonhole. "They won't pat me here."

"But I will." His hand crawls up my leg. "How about we take that off until we are confident we can get past the metal detector and the bouncers?"

"The tights or the camera?"

"The camera."

"It is a bit too cold to take off the tights, isn't it?"

"You sure you're comfortable doing this?" he says, protectively placing his hand on my shoulder, probably sensing that I am in fact rather scared.

"Yes. Of course," I say, because I know that Kevin is excited about this, that this is the kind of work that might give him a thrill. I say yes because I want very badly to be the plucky reporter that I sell myself as, the kind of reporter who would get a thrill from doing things just like this. So I put the camera into his gray canvas knapsack, and we take off in the direction of the neon lights that fill the shadows of Red Square.

The Beverly Hills Casino is owned in part by Chuck Norris, Mr. Law-and-Order himself, and in other parts by the president of the Moscow Gaming Commission, an organization that should raise a few more eyebrows than Bugsy Malone's Vegas joints ever did. For reasons that I cannot even begin to fathom, Chuck Norris is modern Moscow's superstar. Whenever you turn on the television, chances seem to be about 95 percent that you will see that scruffy beard bouncing about the screen. The voice of some monotonal translator is dubbed over the grunts of macho blather that are identifiable in any language, while Chuck karate-kicks his way into some long-legged woman's heart. I get why guys like him. But when I try to understand how such an unattractive man could work his way into any woman's fantasy, I am baffled. The way he wears his jeans, high over his hips and tightly belted around his middle-aged waist, is about as unsexy as the veins popping out of Yeltsin's nose. But they do love Chuck Norris in Moscow, so it is no big surprise that his casino is one of the most popular in town. I find it somehow fitting that the club belonging to this particular Mr. America is situated on the first floor of the looming residential skyscraper that has housed such notable Soviet-era stars as Stalin's hatchet man Lavrenti Beria. And I find it undeniably perfect that the skyscraper is literally within spitting distance of the U.S. embassy.

The driver of the cab that we hitched refuses to bring us to the club's entrance. Not his territory, he explains. So we skate up the dark, icy sidewalk that leads to the monolithic gothic skyscraper, arms locked at elbows for balance and warmth.

"If I go down, you go with me," Kevin says with confidence as we recover from a precarious skid.

I nod. My heart is pounding furiously, and I am afraid that if I speak, my voice might shake, revealing my trepidation. It is so cold that by the time we reach the casino's steps, my jaw and cheeks are frozen shut, and I wonder whether I can talk at all. This doesn't help when the overstuffed bouncer just inside the door tells us to check the bag. I try to explain that I have all sorts of essential feminine products inside, but between my nervous pidgin Russian and ice-locked lips, I sound more like Charlie Brown's teacher than a sultry woman to whom one cannot say no. In the linguistic confusion he lets me pass, bagless and cameraless.

At the next checkpoint (complete with an airport-issue metal detector in the shadows of glossy color photos of Mr. Norris himself), all sorts of bells and whistles sound as we search for the culpable key chain in Kevin's pocket. By the time we get to the third checkpoint, we start to worry that the night is a wash.

"No sneakers," says the man in a shiny black suit who is leaning, legs akimbo and jacket open to reveal a gun, against the last red wall between us and the main gaming room.

"These aren't sneakers." Kevin pulls up a pant leg to reveal a dark green Adidas soccer cleat. He forgot to pack his Doc Martens. The black-suited man grunts and says that we can sit near the dance floor, but that's it. If he sees us at the blackjack table, he says, we'll be booted out. Because Olga works the main floor, we decide to beat him to it. Perhaps another night.

Back we go past checkpoints 2 and 1, grabbing our stuff from the bag check and reemerging into the bitter cold. At the foot of the cement stairs and in the shadow of the embassy, we climb into the back of an idle Zhiguli that is sputtering steam into the cold night air.

Moscow has taxi services, but more often than not the vogue is to hitch a ride in any old car. You are less likely to be ripped off by some guy trying to generate a little extra income than by the notoriously corrupt cabbies in town. So we adjust ourselves onto the cracked vinyl seat.

Kevin leans forward toward the weathered man facing us from the front.

"Rechnoi Vokzal. Festivalnaya Ulitsa," he says, giving the address. They agree on a fee of 50 rubles, which is about $9 and twice the fare we paid to get here.

The man turns around to start the engine, and the car convulses into action, bouncing us back into our seats and forging another embrace.

Kevin kisses my ear.

I smile, relieved to be away from the bouncers and in a warm place.

A moment passes.

"Why aren't we moving forward?" I say, noticing that we are still in front of the casino.

A quiet beat substitutes for any verbal response. It is the sound of metal gently knocking against glass, a blunt object rhythmically tapping the driver's side window. There are probably only two or three taps, but they take place in one of those moments when seconds are drawn through a molasses-saturated version of time. Kevin whispers in my ear that it is a gun. The bouncer is tapping against the window with the barrel of a gun.

The proximity to this potentially deadly object is terrifying, but it quickly becomes exhilarating. The adrenaline blasting through my blood gives me a deep, dazed sense of what immortality must feel like. It feels calm. I want to sit here for a moment, experience it. I want to enjoy not being scared by what I fear. I want to partake in the Chuck Norris movie that seems to be unfolding in front of me.

Kevin doesn't. Suddenly, he's the realist.

"Come on," he says, grabbing my mittened hand and pulling me out of the Zhiguli. As we step out of the passenger side, another couple, a woman in fur and a man in a black woolen coat, climb in from the other. Clearly, they are special VIPs. Their need for a cab takes precedence over ours.

We walk back down the icy path, me trying to watch the proceedings behind us, Kevin pulling me forward. He waves down the next passing car, and I follow him into this automated tin box. Unfazed, he repeats the directions to Rechnoi Vokzal.

People often ask me whether Moscow is a dangerous place to live, and I really don't know how to answer that question. Yes. It depends. It doesn't really matter because I'm a big believer in fate. In the next year I would see many guns and gang shoot-outs. I would hear harrowing stories of rapes and robberies, police brutality and ineptitude. I'd meet people dying of disease, radiation, and random building collapses. I'd read stories in the papers about sidewalks that swallowed people into the boiling rivers of sewage beneath them and of gas leaks in apartment complexes that killed scores of residents. Even when, later, I am the one who is the object of a violent rage, the fear that I feel will be more akin to what one feels in a seat at a multiplex, watching a quick-cut scene in an R-rated movie.

That first Moscow week passes like a film as well. If it were one, right here would be a short montage set to some sappy Slavic tune. Opening shot: Kevin and I are kissing on Red Square. Dissolve to our return to the casino. I roll the dice. Transition to a heated telephone call with my boss. Tight shot of me as I promise to make up for not finding the receipt. Cut to a back-alley chat with Pyotr the Pimp. Cut to a smoky chat around Elena's table. Cut to a silhouetted interview with Olga. Dissolve to a stolen kiss on the metro. Cut to an interview with an obstinate flack at the U.S. embassy. Exit the door at screen left. Dissolve to a tearful goodbye as Kevin gets on the return train to St. Pete. Dissolve to me as I interview for jobs at a variety of network bureaus. Cut to me as I cruise around town with my camera crew, shooting all the typical beauty shots of Moscow: St. Basil's, the Kremlin, the Gagarin statue, kids playing ice hockey, babushkas begging. And before you know it, Elena is stuffing me back onto a plane.

9

NEW YORK—"Hey, I'm home!" I call into the bright foyer of my New York apartment, hoping to find my roommate sprawled on the couch, absorbed in an episode of *Friends*. She isn't around, so I drop my bags at the entrance, toss my keys onto the marble-topped mail table, and make a beeline for the kitchen phone, all while disentangling myself from Ivan, my cat, who is tripping up my legs. I dial, clamping the black cordless under my ear.

"Hey, I'm back!" I say when Erica finally picks up.

"So how was it?" she asks.

I spit out some delirious, excited blather.

"Sounds great, Jen. Congratulations, I guess." She says something about how happy I sound. "But you might want to consider slowing it down a notch."

This makes me bristle. It always has, not just now. People toss out advice like this all the time, advice without perspective, and I am beginning to believe that 90 percent of it is just manufactured out of the fear of having nothing to say. Kind of like justifying a paycheck—people need to give advice, solicited or not, in order to feel valued. I love Erica, but now, when she tells me that I need to consider why I am jumping into this relationship so fast, I have laugh (to myself, of course). It's not like I didn't expect it. In some ways she is obligated to say such things in her role of caring friend. Hell, I would probably say the same if I were on the other end of the line. And the thing is, I think about 90 percent of people who give such advice, Erica included, people who grew up reading fairy tales and seeing Hollywood movies, people who fear loneliness and seek comfort, they would be jumping too, given the opportunity. Please. Consider for a moment the facts and the influences. Everything I have ever wanted or dreamed of is right here in front of me, ripe for the picking. And, good lord, it's not like I am one of those trafficked women, handing my fate to a stranger, watching my babysitting gig turn into a lap dance.

So, anyway, here I am in my kitchen, flipping through the accumulated pile of bills and junk mail, firmly placing Erica in my camp. I tell her about everything. The missionary and the first kiss. The pimps and the prostitutes. The plane rides and the ring.

"Sounds really attractive," she says in her infectious cadence that is part laugh, part speech.

"He promised to get me a real diamond as soon as he has the money," I say. "Actually, I'll probably just give him the money to buy it."

"Now that's romantic."

"Whatever. Anyway, I kind of like this man fucking the air on my finger."

"Really charming."

"But it's abstract enough that it could pass for some expensive piece of Soho art."

"Sure," she says.

"You're happy for me, aren't you? You're happy, right?"

"Yes, Jen. I do think it's kind of great. Honestly. I am happy for you. I don't want you to leave, but I am happy for you."

I have won.

"I love you, Erica," I say and, without so much as a breath to pause, I hang up and dial my parents to tell them with the same hyperactive verbosity that I know that this all seems really fast, but I am quitting my job, moving to Moscow, and marrying a man whom they have never met. No, he isn't Jewish. Not really. But Kevin spent part of his childhood in the predominantly Jewish suburb of Newton, Massachusetts, and that has to count for something.

"Oh, my God," says my mother.

"It's your mother's birthday today," interjects my father.

"Oh, my God," I say.

"Why don't you meet us at the restaurant and we can talk about this over dinner?" says my father.

"Happy birthday, Mom," I say.

"Do you have a picture of this man?" she says.

"Yes."

"Bring it."

When I arrive at the elegant East Side bistro, my brother and his wife are toasting with the first glass of the evening. I sheepishly kiss my mother and crawl into the empty chair.

"How old are you, anyway?" I ask as I unfold the napkin into my lap. If I have inherited my mother's youthful appearance, I will forgive her for handing down all the other quirks.

"You know, I don't really know," she says, touching her bobbed honey-brown hair as if that will provide an answer. "I think I am fifty-seven."

"Mom, you're fifty-six," my brother says. "You were born in forty-two."

"Right, so I'm fifty-seven."

My brother shakes his head in his hands and sighs. We all laugh and try to explain the detail. It takes a moment.

"Oh, my God! But I told everyone at work I'm fifty-seven," she says.

"Maybe by next year they'll forget," says my sister-in-law.

"Or maybe after another year of my shenanigans you'll start to look older," I say, officially handing out the key to Pandora's box.

"It's not all about you, Jennifer," my mother says, and the laughter stops.

But of course it is. Everyone's life is all about himself or herself. That doesn't mean that your concerns are all selfish or that you can't or don't care about others. But in the end it does come back to you, doesn't it? A loved one is sick and you worry about her leaving you. You are sick and you worry about leaving your loved ones. This created a direct relationship between my parents' response to my engagement and the speed with which I let their feelings and my world collide.

It starts like this:

I show them the photo of the man I love and my mother shrieks.

She holds the picture that the babushka shot at the statue of Catherine the Great. Kevin was looking at me as he held me and when the picture came back from the lab, I could feel the affection in his eyes almost as powerfully as if he were there next to me. When asked just who it was I had decided to spend my life with, I thought this was a good photo to show.

The shriek isn't tremendously loud. We are in a restaurant, after all. But it is definitely not a shriek indicative of a calm, thoughtful reaction to my betrothal.

"Oh, my God!" my mother says. Clearly, she is not seeing the same man I see.

"Mom!" I say through my teeth.

"I'm sorry, it's just not what I expected," she says, blushing at the recognition of her own inappropriate behavior. "He just looks a bit odder than I thought."

I wonder just what exactly he should look like in order to merit a more positive response, if nothing short of someone who looks exactly like my brother or father will do, but I don't say anything.

"You have to admit, Jen, he looks strange," says my brother. He is flipping through the rest of the stack of photos I got developed in Moscow. My brother, the tall, dark, and handsome doctor. The doctor with the beautiful wife and beautiful baby girl.

I look to my father (who looks just like my brother), who is always there to back me up.

"I don't mean this the way it will sound," he says, "but Kevin looks a bit like someone who lives abroad because he has to."

"What?"

My father, he's a psychiatrist. "Some people live abroad because they want to," he says, as if this explains anything. "And some people live abroad because they have to. I think you need to figure out what kind of person he is."

"That's ridiculous." I laugh derisively and grab the picture out of my mother's fist. I hold it close to my face. Kevin's eyes are red, but they are loving and kind. His orange knit hat is more like something you might see in some photo essay of the inner city than in the pages of *GQ*, but it is cute. His thick silver rings make him look tough, but I know better. I look down at mine.

"Maybe he does look a bit off," I say, wanting them to understand, wanting this conflict to dissipate, wanting them to comprehend how whole Kevin makes me feel. Wanting to give them the joy that my brother has given them.

I explain the lack of sleep, the exhaustion, and adrenaline. "That's probably what you are seeing," I say.

"Probably. You're right. I'm sorry," says my mother.

"Trust me, you'll love him. I do," I say, reaching across the table to take the rest of the photographs back from my brother.

In the opening sentence of *Anna Karenina,* Tolstoy writes that all happy families are alike and all unhappy families are unhappy in their own special way. It's a famous, oft-quoted line, but it provides no room for that gray middle ground of the moderately happy family, the one where everyone gets along, truly loves each other, but still has some issues to contend with. The neurotic family. The family that loves too much. My family.

It's not that I think that my family's issues are unique, because one fundamental problem with my family is me, and I am nothing special. I am just another single career woman pushing thirty and living in an urban center. And I think that it must be incredibly stressful for any parent of a single career woman who is pushing thirty and living in an urban center. I mean, they too read the recycled urban myth that proclaims that the chance of such a woman's getting married is about as the same as getting run over by an elephant who has escaped from the zoo. And our neighborhood zoo doesn't even have an elephant. But my family has had an elephant in the room for a long time. "What are you doing this weekend?" my mother would ask me over the phone. If I didn't have a date, a party, a possibility, I would try to let her down gently. "Oh, it's no big deal. I really need a quiet weekend, anyway," I would say and then go get a drink with a girlfriend who just said something similar to her parents.

Having an engagement in the works changes the equation. We can become the happily-ever-after family.

As soon as I make my case for how much in love and how very excited I am, pandemonium ensues. I must endure all the variations on "if you love him, that's what matters. He must be wonderful," et cetera and so forth, and soon apologies are gushing forth from all sides. Faster than it takes the waiter to bring on the dessert, my parents have switched from carrying on in horrific disgust to planning a wedding. Not that there is a lot of planning left to be done. Apparently, they have been dreaming it up ever since Gideon Rubin, my kindergarten sweetheart, announced that he would marry me, and that the ceremony would take place in the middle of the West Side Highway. Twenty-five years later all we need to do is paint by the numbers.

Kevin is a bit keener on the idea of getting married at city hall or in Vegas, but it doesn't take much to get him to agree to a real wedding. Rather, it doesn't take much for my enthusiasm to drown out his reservations, even long distance. He already had one wedding, after all. This is going to be my one and only. And, perhaps more to the point, it is going to be the one and only time that my parents can send their daughter off.

"Just tell me where to show up," Kevin says.

I call my folks to see what they think.

"Your father has been planning this since you were a baby," my mother tells me. "He won't admit it, but he has."

"You are going to have to rein your mother in," says my father. "She might try to go a bit overboard with this one."

I say that I am happy to give her the reins.

Come to think of it, rein-holding issues, issues about control, are common among many not-perfectly-happy American families. Take eating disorders, for example. Lots of mildly happy families deal with them in some capacity. And the conventional wisdom about eating disorders is that they are all about control. Familial control. Mother-daughter control. It's not a fool-proof theory; other things are undeniably at stake, especially when we are talking about American teenage girls. Certainly, you don't see Afghan girls binging and purging under their burkas, and, for that matter, bulimia is only just starting to take hold in post-totalitarian Russia. Self-induced vomiting and starvation are luxuries of the well-to-do. But the terms don't translate very well. In high school and college I had an eating disorder, and in the middle of it, in that summer of carnal lust in Leningrad, I tried to explain my problem to my friend Vera. After a few minutes I gave up. "I have something like tapeworm," I finally said. "Sometimes it makes me really hungry, so I eat too much and then I can't keep it down." She suggested that I take an antibiotic, and I changed the subject. But the thing was, in Russia it really was a foreign problem. It was for me, I mean. I didn't struggle with it there. Granted, it was difficult to binge when it was such a headache to gather food in the first place. But later, when breadlines faded into memories and fruit stands started to overflow, my head stayed out of the toilet. After a few college summers in the USSR, I kept it out. Part of that was probably due to the Prozac, part of it to just growing up, but I have to believe that more was going on. Maybe the distance and cultural divide were giving me the autonomy that I needed. Maybe the grittiness of Russia distracted me from whatever it was that drove my fist down my throat in the first place. As the daughter of a psychiatrist and a psychotherapist, good lord, I should be able to figure it out. But theorizing can be tedious, and I would just prefer to accept that I can eat happily and heartily now, thank you very much, and, forgive the double entendre, purge the past.

"Hell," I tell my parents as we discuss the food for the reception, "you can even pick the cake."

They say they are thrilled about this. And they have reason to be. My parents are understandably apprehensive about my jetting off to Russia with a man they have never met. This is not something they can understand or even imagine. But, as stated, my wedding is something they have imagined for years. So we are more comfortable discussing the virtues of fish versus chicken than whether Yeltsin is better than Lebed or Moscow is preferable to St. Pete. If, in our conversations, someone makes reference to Russia, it usually runs along the lines of "why don't you guys spend your first year together in New York and then go travel later on? Russia isn't going anywhere." This invariably unleashes a torrent of bile from my mouth. It is absolutely unimaginable that Kevin and I would do something so dull, I say. The excitement shouldn't have to be so external, they tell me. No, I say, now is the time to go. We'll come back when we are good and ready.

I grant them control over my wedding so I can plan my future.

10

NEW YORK—The few weeks following my mother's birthday meal zipped by at such a frenetic pace that I swear I'm still catching up on my sleep. The office paged me right at the restaurant and sent me off to an undercover shoot involving a gaggle of Russian call girls and probably too many male producers for the job. The developments in the sex-slave story appeased my boss's reactions to the missing Talbott receipt. "You're lucky this story is turning out to be a home run," he said when he called me on my cell phone. "It will be better than that," I answered. A day or so later a district attorney in Brooklyn put me in touch with a detective who put me in touch with Rima, an informant he said owed him a favor. Apparently, this Rima had done a decade or so in a women's prison for stuffing diamonds into the bellies of battered teddy bears and smuggling them out of South Africa. The detective told me that Rima was once a fixture on the Brighton Beach scene, Russian mobsters' hub in the United States. When she wasn't running diamonds, she was running strip bars and escort services.

Rima agreed to meet me at her apartment on an unsavory corner in south Brooklyn.

I take a car service and tell the driver to wait out front.

Rima opens the door for me as if she has been waiting all day. "This is all bullshit," she says, blowing smoke out the side of her mouth. Then she tells me to come in anyway.

I can smell the piss and stale cigarettes before I even enter, and when we do, I almost gag. But I follow her, a pencil-thin blur in black leggings, and sit down on the couch, which was clearly once white but is now gray. I take out a pen and pad.

She offers me Sanka. Her voice is raspy, sandpaperish, making her accent sound too comically criminal to be real, although I suppose it is.

"No, thanks," I say and pick up one of the many pedigreed Persian kittens that are skulking about the place, leaving tracks of fur as they move across the deep wall-to-wall shag carpet, also once white, now gray.

"Want one?" She points her chin at the black cat that has crawled onto my lap. "Uh," I say.

"Anyway," she says, blowing another torrent of smoke that quickly clouds over her face, "there is no fucking Russian Mafia. This isn't Hollywood." She taps a half-inch ash into the overflowing clamshell ashtray that balances precariously on the arm of her love seat; she sits back. As if to accentuate the dramatic pause, the smoke fades away, revealing a frighteningly thin woman with garish red lips and thick strokes of blush that need attention. I would be tempted to lean forward and rub them in if her skin had a texture other than crepe paper. As it is, I am content to keep my distance. She looks like a weathered dominatrix, like a drug-damaged ghost.

"So why did you agree to meet me?" I ask, placing the kitten down on the rug.

"Because Steve told me you're a nice girl." Steve is the detective to whom the DA introduced me. Rima tells me that Steve works for the CIA. "But don't tell him I told you," she says.

"That he said I'm a nice girl?"

She laughs. I laugh too and say something about nice girls being a dime a dozen. She doesn't think it's funny. Instead she changes the subject.

"OK," she says as if I have asked her a favor. Which I suppose I have. She tells me about the Russified strip joints in the south of Brooklyn, which clubs to visit, and what girls to talk to.

I have no idea why Rima tells me what she tells me or what is on her agenda, or what her deal is with Steve, or why Steve would even want to help me out in the first place, but it doesn't really matter. I furiously scribble it all down anyway. Bottom line: I trust these leads on a gut level, which is good enough to send associate producers driving around the tristate area and jetting across the country with hidden cameras strapped inside jackets, hats, and what-have-you. When we shoot the women twirling around poles, gyrating with legs spread, we are so close that we can smell the mustiness emanating from beneath their G-strings. We smile kindly as they thrust their breasts in our direction, hoping one or more of us will place a crisp dollar bill in the elastic. I suppose that the deceit implied by the camera's assumed absence makes me an accomplice to the exploitation that drives this dance, and this thrills me a little. It's as if by being the exploiter, I can't be exploited. The more material I have shot, the more control I have. I rev the hunt for the sexy sex slaves into high gear. While the big boys like *Primetime Live* and their network friends are exposing stories of Russian sex trafficking in Israel and Europe, our scrappy tabloid shop is uncovering the same evidence in our own backyard. My bosses stop mentioning the lost Talbott receipt entirely, stop whining that they don't have enough staff to cover the Clinton scandal, and start mentioning promotions and pay raises.

"We really want you to have a future here, Jen," Bill tells me after he sees a tape that one of our guys shot in a brothel in Maryland.

I blush and blurt out that that is really nice, but I've gotten engaged and am moving to Moscow.

"Can't compete with that," he says, looking a little stunned. "Congratulations."

Starbucks latte in hand and satisfaction in heart, I finish up my work.

During the next two weeks we shoot almost sixty hours of videotape, with both open and hidden cameras; most of it is fairly scintillating stuff. All of it needs to be logged, scripted, edited. Boiled down. I turn on the playback machine and stick in something that was taped while I was on a different shoot. We scored an open-camera interview with a Russian call girl who claimed to fit the profile. She said she had been duped into believing that she would be working as a babysitter, but as soon as her plane hit John F. Kennedy International Airport, her handlers took her passport and forced her into an endless nightmare of striptease and turning tricks. A Russian-speaking camera operator did the interview. He did a stellar job of lighting the woman, really, but his tool for loosening her up was something along the lines of a bottle of Heineken. I watch the video, and I'm a little disturbed by this slice of ethical neglect, but I suppose paying prostitutes for their time isn't really much better. Anyway, as the tape rolls on, the really disturbing thing is that I can hardly understand a word the girl is saying. As her bottle empties, her language gets cruder. It's not so much that I'm worried about handling Russian street life; it's more that I am a bit concerned about the line on my résumé that says I am a fluent speaker. If I mistranslate this, it will look particularly bad when I am interviewing for jobs in Moscow.

I need help, so I call the most foul-mouthed Russian speaker I know.

"Hey, honey. You busy?"

"Hey," he says in that tone that speaks sonnets.

"Hey," I swoon back. Then I explain the situation. He says he has spent enough time in Russian AA meetings and drunk tanks to pick up more than his share of colorful language.

"Play it for me," he says.

I boost up the volume, holding the phone to the monitor.

"Good God!" he says. "That girl talks like a suicidal sailor."

"What did she say?"

"Play it again."

I do.

"I can't even say those words in the office," he says when she's done.

"Oh, come on."

"Look. You know what we do when we lie in bed? Well think of that three times over and inside out in the wrong direction with someone you hate."

"Oh. Probably not a good bite for TV anyway, huh?"

"Probably not. But, hey. Good timing on the call, though. I was waiting to call until it was solid, but—"

"What?"

"Possible great news."

"What? Did you hear from AP?"

"No, no. I asked my boss about sending me to New York to do your trafficking story for the paper."

"Get out! What did he say?"

"He said he thinks it's a go but needs to clear it with Derk."

"Derk?"

"The publisher."

"This is great. Our whole courtship can be subsidized by our employers."

"It's all in the name of journalism." He laughs that infectious laugh. "Put us together and Pulitzer won't know what hit him."

"He's dead, dear."

"I know." He laughs again.

"And he was insane."

"All the better." We giggle.

"OK," I say, "I gotta go."

"I'll call when I hear from Mark."

"Mark?"

"My boss."

"Good deal. I'm going to call Elena and have her translate this all properly from the privacy of her living room."

I call Elena, who says Kevin is correct in his assessment of the call girl's slang, but in the end the bite reads "it sucks" and we beep out the word *suck* because, although it really does suck, you can't say that on television.

N EW YORK — It is true, that adage that if you want to get something done, you should give it to a busy person. But the chances of completion are even greater if that busy person is flying around on an ecstatic high. Right now, I am bouncing off walls, and the only time I can peel myself down is when Kevin finally crawls into my New York bed. For such loquacious lovers our sex life is remarkably silent. We lie here for hours just holding each other, mouths caressing limbs with tender kisses. He gets up and wraps the white sheet around him to get us some water, and as I hear his bare feet padding through the rooms of the apartment, I smile at the thought that the place is now ours, not just mine.

"What do you think about my dowry?" I say when he returns and hands me the sweating glass of cold water.

"I'm just loving being in your space," Kevin says as he climbs back into bed. "Your space makes me feel strong." He gently kisses my shoulder, holding me tight inside his wiry arms.

He got here last night, after convincing his editor to send him stateside so he can do the sex-slave story for his paper. And when we finally emerge from bed, I hand over my sources and we retrace my steps with Rima and the strip joints. He meets my parents, who are immediately infected by our bliss. "He reminds me of David," says my mother, referring to an old family friend, a journalist, who died years before. David was the keystone of our Upper West Side Jewish community when I was growing up, and for my mother to say something like that is better than giving an endorsement; she has awarded a badge of honor. We go down to D.C. so Kevin can interrogate Immigration and Naturalization Service officials, and I introduce him to Erica. "You have never looked so happy," she says. We call his mother. "He's never sounded so good," she tells me. My mother and I get measured for silk wedding dresses, and my father and I reserve an evening at a lovely country inn. "October thirty-first seems like an appropriately quirky date for your wedding," he says when we discover that Halloween is the only date available. "We can have a masquerade ball," I say, really liking the idea.

Date set, Kevin and I start to jet back and forth between Moscow, St. Petersburg, and New York so many times that I honestly can't recall the number of trips we each take. But I have my frequent flier miles to attest that this is all actually happening. In less than three weeks I find a renter for my room, line up a freelance gig in Moscow with the news agency WTN, and start my goodbyes. My piece airs to backslapping ratings and starts speculation about awards and honors. Kevin's editor sends the articles to my fax machine, and we are trembling and giddy as we relive our reporting through his prose.

RUSSIAN SEX SLAVERY 'EPIDEMIC' IN U.S.
Editor's Note: This is the first in a series of three articles.

By Kevin Dillard
staff writer

BROOKLYN, New York—Somewhere beyond the smoky spotlights at a go-go club on Coney Island Boulevard, waiting for her next routine, Marina, a raven-haired 23-year-old native of Moscow, adjusts her G-string and calculates the money she'll make tonight.

It's brutally precise math she has learned while working for almost two years as a sexual slave after answering a vague yet intriguing ad she found in a Moscow newspaper.

81

"Earn thousands of dollars a month working abroad in a dance troupe," the ad had read. A month and a half after calling the phone number—and passing an audition that included stripping to a tape of Duran Duran on a tinny boom box—Marina was living in a run-down Brooklyn apartment with 12 women, four beds, barred windows and almost daily beatings.

A few days later, back in St. Petersburg, Kevin's yellow Soviet phone is ringing off the hook.

"I have another interview at *Newsday*," he tells me over the clackity-clack of the line. I am still in New York, tying up loose ends.

"Get out!" I say, switching the receiver to my more attentive ear.

"Seriously. They need an acting bureau chief for the summer."

"Get the fuck out. And they want you?"

"Shocking, isn't it?"

"Actually, no. Not shocking at all. You're a genius."

He laughs, but it's true.

"But did you agree on an end date with Matt?"

"He wants me to stay through May."

"What?"

"It's not that long."

"But you are getting offers in Moscow now. And I can't get work in St. Pete."

"I owe them."

"You don't owe them shit."

"They let me do the sex story in New York."

"They let you? It's the best article that's run in that fucking rag of a postcollegiate paper since it started."

"It's not a fucking postcollegiate rag."

"But it's not a gig as the chief at *Newsday*, either."

"That's not solid. And it's only for the summer. And it hasn't been offered yet."

"Jesus. You'd make more selling one article to a magazine than you do in a year working for your paper. I thought you said you would move to Moscow as soon as I can get my ass over there."

"Well, maybe I'm not ready to get my ass over there yet," he says, and I fall silent, not knowing what to say to that.

12

Moscow—I suppose there comes a point in every new relationship when tensions swell a bit, causing small stress fractures in the metaphorical glass slipper. But something about our discord actually makes everything feel safe, more established and adult, if you will. It makes it real. Kevin knows it too. We actually talk about it and kind of agree that we will deal with all the problems later or that maybe they will just work themselves out, once our whiplash from the whirlwind settles, now that the trafficking story has been put to bed. Right now, it's time to phase into our next story, to change our narrative just a bit. Because the thing is, I already have the plane tickets, the renter, and the plans. And so, not two weeks after he has told me that he is feeling apprehensive about leaving his friends and support network in St. Petersburg, we are again crashing at Elena and Mikhail's, stomping around the icy puddles that lace Moscow's cracked cement sidewalks. We sign a lease on a small ground-level apartment near the zoo and are running from interview to interview as if we are on a junket. He's been to all the major papers, and my appointment calendar looks like *TV Guide:* ABC, NBC, CBS. It seems everyone wants a piece of us.

Pinch me, I think.

Kevin is waiting for me as I walk away from the CNN bureau, out of the complex on Kutuzovsky Prospect that houses a plurality of the foreign bureaus in town, past the armed guards and onto the street. He is wet from the frozen drizzle, but he's smiling, suppressing laughter, like he is overjoyed just to see me jump over a puddle. He catches me as I trip into his arms and kisses me with his smoky lips.

"Well?"

"Not bad," I say. CNN seems like a real possibility, but I don't want to jinx it.

"What do you mean, not bad? Didn't they love you?"

I sigh with exaggerated exasperation and express my concern that not everyone loves me at first contact the way he had but that it seems hopeful nonetheless.

"We had a nice conversation," I say.

"What about?"

I tell him that the bureau chief seems to be a bit fixated on the emergence of Russia's middle class. That she thinks that we've all been missing that, the big story.

"That there is a real middle class emerging in Russia?"

"Right."

He throws back his head and cackles. "Good God! What an idiot. How long has she been here?"

"Not long enough, I guess." I guess. She seemed smart to me.

"Or too long. She needs to get her fucking head out of this asinine expat-villa."

"Oh, and then there was this." I hand Kevin a sheet of wire copy that the bureau chief printed out for me. "It pretty much ended the interview."

MOSCOW (AP)—Russian President Boris Yeltsin fired his prime minister and the entire government in a bombshell announcement Monday that stunned the nation.

"Holy shit!" he says before he finishes reading the first sentence. He reads the rest, kind of cursing and muttering as he goes, and grabs my wrist.

"I have to catch the midnight train back to St. Pete," he tells me, breathless.

"But we need to be in New York next week," I say, trying to keep up as he pulls me through the gauntlet of people and potholes leading to the metro. "Our plane is in two days." The movers are coming to put my things in storage. Our friends are throwing us a party on Friday.

"I'll meet you there when the story settles. I'm still the fucking news editor until the end of the month, you know."

"This story isn't going to settle anytime soon," I am saying as we run through the closing door of the subway car. "And, anyway, it's happening in Moscow."

He ignores me and says he has to get to the station by ten, which gives us time for a nap. All the other details will sort themselves out. They always do. And I suppose he is right. It would look bad for him not to be covering this story, not to end his career at his paper with a bang.

We exit the subway and step off the rickety escalator and into the mud-covered market square at Rechnoi Vokzal. Drunken men are pissing behind magazine kiosks and tough-looking leather-clad teenagers are standing around the beer concessions with nothing to do.

Kevin tugs me through the frozen drizzle, navigates the labyrinth of babushkas selling dried flaking fish and cheap toilet paper. A policeman steps in front of us, cutting us off.

He is young, maybe twenty. And he has an enormous gun holstered against one leg.

"*Vashi dokumenty,*" he demands. Your documents.

I fumble for mine.

"Don't," Kevin says, knocking my hand out of my coat pocket. I look at him, stunned.

The policeman repeats himself.

"Under what code?" Kevin asks, aggressively. In Russian. "You have no right to ask us for our papers without reason. Give me the reason."

The cop, the boy, says nothing.

"You have no fucking reason," Kevin tells him and pulls me away. "I am so fucking sick of that shit," he says. I look back and see the cop watching us, frozen still, a toy soldier with a real weapon.

My heart is in my throat. "Are you crazy?" I say.

"What?" Razor tongued, it feels like a snake bite. He says I need to trust him. That he has been living in this country for years, I haven't. That I don't know what I am doing.

I pull my wrist out of his grip and stop walking. Our eyes catch and I can see him seeing me, seeing my face drain, my throat lump up.

"I am so sorry," he says and takes me into his chest.

"That scared me," I say.

"It's OK," he whispers. "It's going to be great." He kisses my forehead, my watery lashes. My lips.

We turn the corner, enter Elena's building, go into the apartment. We toss off our wet shoes and clothing and crawl under the soft folds of the blankets and sheets. Elena and Mikhail have turned the master bedroom over to us again while they spend the week sleeping on the stained rug in the baby's room. We burrow into their marital mattress, still something of a luxury in the post-Soviet world, cover ourselves with the *odeialo*—a scratchy wool blanket tucked into a duvet cover for softness and warmth—cradle each other's chilled bodies, and promptly fall into our dreams.

I should have seen the signs. Perhaps I did see them but didn't want to recognize them in my waking life. My dreams are fitful and frightening. Lots of strange, unfamiliar characters and cold damp rooms. I have dreams of being chased out of AA meetings and others of being chased into them. I dream about death and about slow, tortured murders. Unlocatable babies crying. Cavernous labyrinths lacking in oxygen. The dreams are seemingly endless, each dripping with more clichéd symbolism than the last, but in my waking hours I don't really think about them.

The signs are here, though. Clear as vodka.

For the past two days we've been traipsing around Moscow, and for the past two days I've been smelling stale alcohol. I tell myself that it is the smell of Russia. If that smell rubbed off on Kevin's scent-absorbing jacket, what fault of his is that? But just to be sure, I ask him about it.

We are sitting on the metro, coming back from the outdoor pet market where we had purchased a comically large kitty litter box in celebration of signing the lease. If we're going to have a Western-style toilet (instead of the ubiquitous but practically powerless Soviet variety), Kesha should have one too. No more torn newsprint in a milk crate.

I rest my feet on the box in front of us and place my head on Kevin's cracked suede shoulder.

I sniff. "Do you smell that?"

"Smell what?"

"It smells like alcohol." I wrinkle my nose.

"Sweetie, we're in Russia."

"No. It smells on your jacket."

Kevin bristles and gets a little defensive. "It probably smells on you too, you've just become numb to the scent."

"You haven't been drinking, have you? Don't get mad. I just have to ask."

"No, silly," he says, not mad. "I haven't had a drink in three years."

That is enough. I nestle further into the hard dirty jacket and close my eyes until we reach our stop.

But it wasn't just the smell.

Since we arrived in Moscow this time around, Kevin has been popping Valium the way I pop gum when my mouth is sour. We can't walk past an *apteka* (drugstore) without at least inquiring about the sedatives available. Just like sidewalk pushers, the buxom lab-coated babushkas who run the pharmacies will dole out anything if the price is right. Valium isn't a controlled substance in Russia, but I don't know what else Kevin acquires from the old ladies. I don't ask. He says he suffers from panic attacks, and this is a stressful time. Between the travel, the job interviews, the apartment hunts, the social calls, and back to the job interviews, we have had no time to process anything. I let the sedative problem slide. I try to ignore his

88

erratic behavior. If I can take my meds, he can take his. And when we are lying in bed and snuggling, there are no problems at all.

None.

I am getting married. We are going to have a fascinating life together. I am not going to be a lonely old maid. My parents will dance at my wedding. I am going to have an important and exciting career. My dress will be lovely. My husband will win Pulitzers. I am going to have a diamond on my finger. I am real.

I awake in a puddle of sweat.

Kevin isn't here.

And when I stumble into the potato-steamed kitchen, blinking to remoisten the dried-up contacts glued to my eyes, I don't see him.

"*Gde* Kevin?" I ask Elena with my heavy accent. Where is Kevin?

"He went to get cigarettes," Elena says in perfect Russian. She looks up from the aluminum pot she's stirring and points the soup-coated ladle at me. "Oh, and Jessica Sanders called you from Fox News." The bureau chief. I have been playing phone tag with her for a few days now. "She said it's important."

"Fabulous." I run to get my Filofax. I search the bedroom. It isn't on the table. It isn't on floor. Right. I gave it to Kevin to carry.

I open up his gray canvas knapsack and I know I won't be calling Fox today.

I see it at the bottom of the bag a nearly empty bottle of the cheapest vodka a ruble can buy. It is lying sideways atop my date book.

"Fuck," I say aloud but under my breath. If Kevin is going to be such an asshole and drink, it's totally pathetic that he is drinking this Drano and not something even mildly smooth. "What a jerk," I think.

And then I think about the lease. The plans. The dress. The hope. The lies.

I drop the bag, and the bottle rolls onto the floor. I crawl back into bed, catatonic. A few minutes later I feel the cold air that he carries in from the street, but I don't look up.

"Hey," he says. I hear him kicking off his shoes.

89

I don't respond.

"What's wrong?"

I want to cry, but I can't. I want to scream, but I lie silent.

He walks closer, tripping over the glass bottle before he reaches the bed.

"Don't bother picking it up," I say. "It's empty."

He picks it up.

He defends it all admirably, in a way that would melt the heart of any woman. It was only because he is so happy, so in love and so hopeful, that he felt strong enough to drink again, he says. He wanted to find out if he could handle the alcohol well enough to have wine at our wedding. He wanted to be normal for me. He made a mistake. He was wrong. He is sorry. He can't promise that he will never drink again, but he will never lie to me. Ever. And drinking behind my back is a lie.

"You never did have the Talbott receipt, did you?"

"Fuck," he says, "Of course I did." He tells me again about how the whore gave it to him, about how, for a while, he even had it pinned on the bulletin board at work.

I remain silent under the covers and listen. I have no choice but to trust him. We have just put more than $2,000 of my money into the new apartment. I quit my job. I sublet my place in New York. I tortured my family with my plans of departure and delighted them with the comfort that I would be married. I jumped off a cliff, and I have to land somewhere. We have such potential. Our life, if we want, can be passionate and grand. I have to believe that. I have nothing else.

"OK," I say. "Are you still going to St. Pete tonight?"

"I have to."

He crawls under the *odeialo* with me and I close my eyes.

13

NEW YORK—I go back to New York for the last time, and for the first time in my life, I don't tell anyone anything. Life, I like to say, is in the telling. If I don't tell, it never happened, there is no script. And anyway, if there were a script, it would be sitting in Russia. And no one at home reads Cyrillic.

"Ariel Goldstein had a fabulous band at her wedding," my mother says.

"Salmon or chicken?" asks my father.

We are sitting around the glass coffee table in my folks' living room, poring over the glossy catalogue that the inn sent us with the wedding package, sorting through the options, checking off lists and drawing up charts. It feels like I am filling out one of those quizzes that they have in *Cosmo* or *Glamour:* If I check one box, it will show that I am a type-A freak, but another box will show just how down-to-earth I am.

"Whatever you guys want," I say, meaning it, because what I really want is their wedding. My parents were married at the Forest Hills Synagogue in Queens, where my mom grew up. It was the Fourth of July, 1966, and it was about 104 degrees outside. The air conditioner broke down midceremony, taking with it everyone's inhibitions. By the middle of the evening people were dancing tie-less, shoeless, shirtless. A bacchanalian brouhaha, a celebratory schvitz. I love that, the unaffected passion that laces through my parents' lives, the jubilance they occasionally let out. I don't see it often, but every now and then they dance barefoot in the kitchen. On summer nights they hold court on the porch of their country house, drinking wine with friends and telling stories. Sometimes my father laughs so hard that tears roll down his face. My mom rolls her eyes, but you can tell that she is loving it.

"How about a little klezmer during cocktails?" says my father. Klezmer is Jewish folk music.

"Oh, this is going to be so much fun," says my mom.

And it is. It is fun right now. Maybe this is really the moment I have dreamed of. Maybe, when dreaming about diamonds and white dresses, what I was really dreaming about was the pride that my folks would feel when they looked at me as I walked down the aisle and the pride I would feel when I looked at them. It was a dream about giving them something joyous, wonderful. This isn't a family therapy session to deal with my bulimia, like in college; it isn't a meeting to speak with my high school guidance counselor or a session with the accountant to figure out how to pay back my loans. It's more like a present to my parents for putting up with all that.

The turbulence at the Kremlin pretty much guarantees me and Kevin any job we want. Russia is once again on page one of the *New York Times,* and that means all the networks suddenly think the story is worth covering. *Newsday* is clamoring for Kevin to start earlier, and the *Moscow Times* anoints him head of the political desk.

"How are you going to swing both jobs?" I ask when he calls to tell me the news. He is still in St. Pete but is about to come to New York, just in time to help me leave properly. In time for the final going-away party.

"I'll be covering the same shit, won't I?"

"Hmmm." I think about it for a moment. I guess it's doable. And I'll be covering the same shit. We agree that we can help each other out.

My other line clicks in.

"Hold on one sec," I say, leaving Kevin to listen to a void three thousand miles away. When I finally click back, it's my turn to lay on the news.

"Oh my God!" I say.

"What?"

"That was the head of one of the networks' foreign desks. I have another interview tomorrow." I exhale. "Oh, my God, I want this."

"You'll get it."

I ignore him and proceed to freak out. My Russian is rusty. My reporting skills are stale. I don't know the ins and outs of the story. I don't have enough experience to be a network news producer. *Breaking Story* is tabloid crap—who am I to think I can do this?

"Sweetie?"

"What?"

"You're insane."

"Maybe I should just jump on a plane and take a bath in your tub for the rest of my life."

"You'll be fine."

"Hold on."

"What are you doing?"

"Shuffling my tarot deck."

I flip a dozen or so cards until I get enough satisfying answers:

NINE OF CUPS: HAPPINESS—Complete success. Pleasure and happiness. Physical well-being. An assurance of a successful future.

THE MAGICIAN—The ability to turn ideas into actions, handle problems, and control one's life. Also the beginning of a new project or direction of life.

THE FOOL—A person vulnerable because of being immature and having unrealistic ideals but who can achieve things with cunning and charm. It may also signify that an important choice needs to be made. "Look before you leap" as the saying goes. Inquirer should avoid becoming obsessed with someone or something; keep a sense of proportion.

We laugh at the last one, and I let Kevin off the line. He promises to e-mail me words of encouragement and love. I tell him to send me something that I can print out and put in my pocket. That way, when I feel nervous, I can touch the paper and be soothed.

The e-mail is waiting for me when I get out of bed the next morning.

TO jcohen@yahoo.com
FROM kdillard@spbpress.ru
SUBJ The Network
DATE March 25, 1998
Dear Dear Dear:

You are stressing. So am I. Remember that tarot reading that said the key to scoring a new job is to be totally charming. This, for you, is no problem. No problem at all. Do you realize how charming you are, what kind of people skills you have, how you can work a room and leave everyone at ease? Perhaps I only notice that because I have such a deficit of these people skills. My routine diplomacy includes saying such things to my underlings as "will you please fuck off? I'm in the middle of a million different things and I'm not even sure we're going to run that crappy story of yours anyway." The coup de grace, however, was when Mark and the publisher Derk wanted to talk to me this morning about the Moscow move. I was deep into a Kirinyenko editorial and didn't want to be bothered. Matt came up behind me and asked for a word. My response, without looking up, was "what the fuck do you want? can't you see I'm busy?" Then I turned around and saw Derk. My face fell.

"Don't apologize," he said. "You just have balls." To kiss his ass I apologized profusely in my broken Friesian Dutch. He responded, also in Friesian, to say, "No offense taken. Balls, when they are not big, don't work so well. Keep up the good work." So that's just a long way of saying I have no people skills and admire yours, which are honed to perfection. So, if the tarot is right, I think you're in like Flynn.

Some stories you might want to pitch him are the recent switch of nuclear ministers. Old story newswise, but it goes deeper than that. I warn you that this is a story I have been smoking out for the past two years, but I'll let The Network have it once I've run it and once they have paid a tidy consulting fee for my sources. The idea, in any case, is to get you in the door with a hot job, after which they may even forget about the story.

Story ideas:

* Basically the Russian government is engaged in a garage sale of its rundown nuclear technology to whoever will buy it. The biggest customers so far are China and Iran. I have all the contacts and sources you need, but I warn you, this would fall under the category of stories that will get you whacked.
* Another one that could get you whacked is an investigation of the fleecing of the IMF [International Monetary Fund] money. You are aware that any money that comes into Russia goes right back out into some sneaky bank accounts belonging to various politicos and businessmen, right? I have sources that could basically write you an itinerary that would wind up at some offshore banks near Cyprus and probably back in the States as well. I've wanted to do this story for a long time (possibly even a book), but without Network-like resources, it's just a pipe dream.
* A wrap on Chechnya today. I could show you around. And it needs to be done. The place has gone to hell. Mark is thinking of sending me anyway. We could go together. Imagine making love amid the rubble. . . .
* And yes, my baby, the nuclear waste dumps in the middle of big cities. Be minimalist about this because I don't want them sending a camera crew up here over the weekend. Tell them, vaguely, that you know of several radioactive waste

dumps in several major Russian cities. Don't even mention St. Pete. Tell them they'll get the story, locations, cancer rates, etc., when they hire you. In any case, I am the only person in the world who knows about it at the moment—at least as it concerns St. Pete—and if I get some call from the network bureau in Moscow before you have been hired with benefits, I will give them a list of fifteen contact numbers that I will make up on the spot and charge them a $1,000 consulting fee for each one.

Anyway, this is just a number of things that none of these hacks knows about and that you can exploit to your advantage during the interview. I will send this off via e-mail shortly, but I wish I could send you more, like a kiss, a surreptitious little cop between your legs, the pressure of my hard-on against your thigh, the mind-shuddering split as I enter you, the collapsed exhaustion of coming together.

Jennifer, I love you.

I close down my computer, put on my Bebe pantsuit, and head off for the interview.

I get the job. It's a local hire position, meaning no expat perks like a big Western apartment, health benefits, or 401(k)s, but the salary is good and, bottom line, I'm going to be a network producer in a foreign bureau. Start date: the day after we arrive in town, two days after our farewell party in Manhattan.

I sit on my bed with my cat in my lap and shuffle the deck one more time. I pull the judgment card and I laugh.

JUDGMENT—A final decision in respect of the past. The taking of a definite step. A change from a totally personal point of view to one that is aware of the cosmic influences. A time of atonement, healing and fulfillment. Overcoming negative situations and the problems associated with them.

14

NEW YORK—There are a variety of ways to travel between Moscow and New York. You can fly nonstop on Delta, through Helsinki on Finnair, through Paris on Air France. Or you can fly direct on Aeroflot. Aeroflot is the cheapest option, and in many ways it's not as bad as you might think. In order to fly in and out of JFK, the planes have to fit a quasi-comforting American standard, so Aeroflot's international craft are, at least where it counts, identical to Delta's. But on Aeroflot, more often than not, you will have a nearly empty flight and get to spread out on three seats for the price of one. That said, seat selection doesn't happen until you check in, and if you unwittingly get a crowded flight, you stand a good chance of being relegated to the smoking section. I have one particularly indelible memory of being sandwiched between two large chain-smoking men. One had the decency to smoke Marlboros, but the other insisted on his native Byelomore Canals, the filter of which is fashioned out of a hollow white cardboard tube that is loosely connected to a funnel of waxy paper holding in blackened soot that masquerades as tobacco. The brand is named after one of Stalin's work projects, a canal built by prisoners from the local gulag, hundreds of whom died during the digging. To the untrained nose the smell of a lit Byelomore Canal is indistinguishable from burned plastic.

Kevin acquired a taste for Byelomores while living in St. Petersburg, so he always lobbies for the smoker-friendly Aeroflot flights. And, he argues, given the Soviet-era service and the inedible food, Aeroflot cushions the culture shock. I agree. I like to think of an Aeroflot ride as an eight-hour immersion course in language and culture, whichever direction you are headed. Beyond that, for a nicotine-sucking, tar-puffing addict like Kevin, Aeroflot is a life preserver. But the airline doesn't take my frequent flyer miles, so this time around, for the final back and forth, Kevin will have to endure a Delta flight to New York.

"Just sleep," I tell him over the phone line. "Take some melatonin."

"Couldn't you at least have gotten me a stopover somewhere?"

"My miles are on Delta."

"Finnair takes their miles."

"But we are flying back on Delta. I really don't want a layover when we are transporting my entire life. We've been through this."

"I wish you had FedEx-ed some nicotine gum."

"You didn't ask."

"This is going to suck."

"It's nine hours, honey. You sleep that long without smoking, don't you?"

"And you know what I look like in the morning."

"You look delicious in the morning."

"That's only because you haven't put on your contacts yet."

"Whatever. Look, it's just nine hours. Sleep. Take a few pills. You'll be fine."

"OK. I'll meet you at the gate," he says and asks if I could try to cop a few Valium to ease the arrival. He's run out again.

"I'll be there. Isn't that enough?" I say and joke that I will bring some more Valium if he can promise he'll have a real engagement ring for me.

"That's supposed to be a surprise, love. But maybe I will have something."

"Well, maybe I'll be there, then."

We laugh.

"Silly girl." He sighs, and I can picture him gently shaking his head in mock reprimand. "I adore you," he says.

"I adore you too. I'm not sure I can wait the twelve hours to see you."

"Take a pill and sleep through it."

"Very cute."

"Good night, sweetie."

"Sweet dreams."

Thirteen hours later I'm leaning against the waist-high iron rail that holds the greeters back as the arrivals funnel out of JFK's customs area. The plane is late because of inclement weather in Newfoundland, and people are growing restless.

"Are you waiting for the Moscow flight?" They ask each other.

"Yes," they answer.

"What time is it supposed to arrive?" asks one.

"I thought three o'clock," says another.

"It's three-forty now."

"Maybe they are coming in another gate."

"Wait. Maybe that's them."

I lean farther over the bar. I see Kevin dragging his canvas army surplus backpack like Bam-Bam carries his bat. But, as he gets closer, I notice that he's shaking, trembling like a heroine addict in withdrawal. I quickly scan the hall for the nearest exit that he can use to grab a smoke.

He sees me leaning over the fence. The smile that crosses his face looks a little pained.

"Next time I promise we can fly Aeroflot," I say when he

approaches speaking distance. He manages a weak laugh and falls forward to kiss me.

When you kiss a smoker, you are kissing an ashtray. When you kiss a smoker undergoing withdrawal, you are kissing a sticky cesspool of expurgating phlegm and tar. I push Kevin away and pull him toward the nearest emergency exit as he desperately fumbles in his jacket pockets.

He lights up, and I am almost as relieved as he is.

"This wasn't how I imagined this," he said upon the third exhale, life coming back to his posture, his face.

"Imagined what?"

"This," he says. He tosses the burning cigarette off the curb. We watch the butt land in the gutter and quickly fizzle out.

Kevin takes my hand in his cold sweaty palm.

"I love you," he says and gets down on one knee.

You know what's coming when a guy does that.

I try to fight back my tears. It's futile.

Kevin is saying something, but all I can hear is the sound of cars circling the passenger pickup area. Through the watery blur I see he is searching his jacket pockets again. He drops my hand for a second to speed things up and then picks it back up to slide a ring onto my finger.

The diamonds glisten.

Somehow, amid all the kissing and hugging and blubbering, I say yes. Yes. Again. For real. Yes. A million times over. Yes. And you will never have to fly Delta again. (Note: Aeroflot has since announced a nonsmoking policy on international flights, effective January 1, 2000.)

Sure, we already have a date set, but the diamond makes it real. And although the ring and the proposal aren't exactly what I envisioned in my schoolgirl fantasies, the romance behind them so surpasses anything that I've ever seen in a DeBeer's ad that I immediately forgive the inconsistencies.

The ring is thin, much more delicate than you might imagine, considering that it once was owned by the favorite girlfriend of a

Russian godfather. Unlike the gaudy baubles adorning the mistresses of Russian mobsters, this ring is simple and sweet. Eight tiny diamonds line the top of a simple gold band. They are so small that they barely show under the platinum prongs that hold them down. But they are real; their sparkle breaks through the grips.

Two days later, after the packing sessions and family functions, at the send-off party that Erica and my soon-to-be ex-roommate are throwing for us, I hold out my hand for all to see. Kevin is sitting in my overstuffed armchair, surrounded by our friends and family. Holding court. I am sitting on his lap. My bags and boxes double as extra seats for the guests, and orange juice and seltzer take the place of alcohol.

"Tell them the story," I say, turning toward him.

He laughs and leans forward around me to place his empty plastic cup on the floor. "You sure you want to share this one?" he asks me.

"Are you kidding? It's our best story yet."

"You start. I'm gonna grab a smoke." He gently pushes me off his lap, and I settle into the cushion he has been warming for an hour. "I'll be right back," he tells our guests.

My friends smile at me, nodding with approval as Kevin leaves the room.

The admonitions of "slow down," the concern for my impetuosity—they are replaced with showers of accolades, shadows of envy.

"He's great," they say.

"So charming."

"So funny."

"Maybe I should start contacting all my college crushes," says one friend.

"Seriously!" says another.

"You guys seem so happy," says everyone.

And we are. I am.

Like a professional hand model, I show off the ring one more time.

"I'll start the story," I say.

I explain that we couldn't really afford a diamond ring but that I was adamant that I get one. Poor Kevin had to punt. Lucky for him, he's friendly with a man named Oleg, and it just so happens that this Oleg is the chief of St. Petersburg's anti-corruption task force. And it just so happens that this anti-corruption task force is completely corrupt. When Oleg heard that Kevin was engaged, he called to offer his congratulations. Kevin mentioned his diamond plight, and Oleg said he had just the solution.

"I'll take it from there," says Kevin, reclaiming his spot beneath me. He cradles me in those stringy arms.

"Please do." I pull a box of Altoids from his shirt pocket and place one on his tongue. "You tell it better anyway."

"It really all begins with the Broiler," he says, crunching down on the mint and pausing to make sure he has everyone's attention. He does.

The Broiler was, once upon a time, the godfather of the Velikie-Luki gang. A few months before my meeting Kevin, the Velikie-Luki gang and the Tambovskoe gang were enmeshed in a bloody land grab over some of St. Petersburg's hottest properties. Bodies were falling everywhere, but the Broiler was untouchable. And the longer he lived, the more properties his "family" was able to claim.

Like any proper Mafia don, the Broiler knew how to enjoy his earnings. Each land grab brought him another majestic flat in the city center, each flat dripping with more ostentatious furnishings and priceless paintings than the next. He had dachas on the outskirts of town, jets to play with, servants for every whim and fancy, and, of course, mistresses for every occasion. His favorite mistress was a blond named Marina, a former prostitute and exotic dancer who now spent most of her time flashing her diamonds and furs and zipping around town in the Broiler's Mercedes.

One crisp day this past fall, Marina and the Broiler piled into the back of his newest jet-black Benz. "Nevsky Prospect," he said to the chauffeur as they pulled out of the courtyard. "Versace," said Marina. She wanted a new jacket.

The buffed nose of the car was barely out of the cast-iron gate when a small battalion of masked, camouflaged men descended upon it. In an instant bullets were spraying out of machine guns, and enough grenades were exploding to flatten a small town. Then, just as suddenly, the shots died down and the smoke settled. A momentary stillness shrouded the car, only to be broken seconds later by guttural groans from the backseat. The chauffeur was hemorrhaging from countless wounds. Marina's head was blown straight off her body and into the Broiler's lap. The Broiler was still conscious and breathing. In shock he gingerly lifted his lover's head by its blond mass of hair and placed it in the puddle of blood pooling on her Gucci skirt. Laboriously, he dragged his battered, oozing body out of the backseat and pulled himself around the car, trying to hold steady on his feet. And as he stood there, grasping at the charred, tattered door, his torso undulating like a flag in wind, he noticed an envelope sitting in the middle of the car's smoldering hood.

It took a minute for his trembling hands to hold steady enough to lift the envelope and pull out the document inside.

It was a one-way ticket to Bulgaria.

He took the ticket and hasn't been heard from since.

As he tells this story, Kevin searches the room with his eyes the way a camp counselor might while telling ghost stories around a fire.

"Get out!" says one friend.

"That can't be true," says another.

"And what the hell does that have to do with Jen's ring?"

"I'm getting there," says Kevin. "And yes, it is all true."

"How do you know?"

"I covered it for the paper." Everyone nods submissively. "But let me go on," he says.

The officers of St. Petersburg's anticorruption task force were ridiculously underpaid, if they were paid at all. To make ends meet, or even overlap, some guys developed the habit of confiscating items from crime scenes. Evidence. The evidence was stored in the back of their headquarters and periodically sold off or even given away to potentially helpful personages. The short story is that, instead of a Tiffany box, my ring came wrapped in a tiny Ziploc bag, the kind the dealers use when selling pot or crack. It had slipped quite easily off the whore's rigid finger and onto my shaky one.

"That's disgusting," says one friend.

"I hope you had it cleaned," says another.

"I think it's fabulous," I say. "So much better than some sterile pronged thing." I proudly hold it up again. "I love it."

I show it proudly for a while, but the funny thing is, sometimes when I look at it, I feel like I am committing a crime. Which is rather intoxicating, I think.

15

N EW YORK — Keflex
Claritin
Diflucan
Xanax
Sominex
Durex
Ibuprofen
Cephalexin
Relafen.

Prozac. A year's supply. My doctor gave me his freebie sample stock as a goodbye present, and I am now sitting in the middle of my bedroom floor, popping the small green and cream-colored pills out of the foil-backed cards and into an old translucent brown plastic container that once held penicillin. The rest of the drugs, stuff I unloaded from my medicine cabinet, my drawers, my parents' closet, are scattered around me, waiting to be sorted and packed.

"Make sure you bring extra in case I need some," Kevin says, and I toss an emptied Prozac card at him. He blocks it with a midair slap of his hand. It volleys back in my direction, falling near my foot. I kick it under the radiator.

"Honey," I say coquettishly, "I'll share my life with you, but I won't share my vitamin P."

"Vitamin P?"

"I take it with my One-A-Day Multi Tab."

"Cute."

"Anyway, I thought you said you got some Zoloft out of your mom's medicine cabinet."

"No. I said she once took all my Zoloft out of my medicine cabinet."

"She took your Zoloft?"

He raises his eyebrows in acknowledgment.

I shake my head and return to popping the pills out of the backing. My future mother-in-law. His mom. Rebecca Dillard. She is a language professor at our alma mater, which was the only reason why Kevin was there and not at Harvard or Yale. Children of professors got free rides with room and board back when Kevin and I met in Dobrak's office.

Kevin's mother was one of the most popular professors on campus, and she looked very much the part. She wore her dark blond wavy hair loose and luminous down her narrow back and had a perpetually plaintive expression across her porcelain face. A tremendously beautiful and enigmatic woman, Rebecca Dillard held the hearts and ruled the dreams of all heterosexual male language majors and not a few faculty members. And if you believed the campus gossip, one or two had had their hands full of her. Once I asked Kevin how many lovers he thought his mother had gone through, and he laughed and said they were neck and neck in the competition. He told me he had slept with more than sixty women when he lost count. Another thing he said that he shared with his mom was her mildly depressive tendencies. He said they were under control and not really at a clinical level, and, sure, she's been known to steal his Zoloft from time to time, but there is nothing really wrong with this since sometimes he stole other things from her.

I suppose this all should have shocked me. Perhaps a light bulb or two should have gone on in my head. But the truth is that I find a great deal of comfort in the Dillard family *mishegas*. I like the Tolstoyan uniqueness of their difficulties. And, not to go off on some self-absorbed Elizabeth Wurtzel/*Prozac Nation*-like tangent or anything, but I do understand. Torment is a status symbol these days, and Rebecca Dillard wears hers well. It is glamorous, a mysteriously seductive torment that draws the concerned affections of men and women alike. You can see it in her eyes. You can almost smell it.

The first time I met her was at the graduation party that she threw for Kevin back in '92. I remember the lumpy pink lox spread and the cheap champagne. The first time I am introduced to her as my future mother-in-law, it is six years later at 11:30 on a frigid Tuesday night, two days before Kevin and I are to take off for good. We meet at a twenty-four-hour French bistro near Gramercy Park, a place where pierced college students sit hip to hip with second-tier models and the men who like to be seen with them. It is the kind of place one often winds up at, late on a weekday evening in lower Manhattan. It is not the kind of place I would have imagined meeting my mother-in-law, but Rebecca is in town to guest lecture at NYU this evening and it seemed to her as good a place as any. Kevin's twenty-year-old acting student–sister, Delia, recommended it. Delia clearly understands her mother, because Rebecca seems completely at home here. When we walk in, she is nursing a scotch and ice, while Delia is lighting her cigarette off the burning butt in her mother's hand.

"Hey!" Rebecca sings out upon seeing us and jumps up to give her older child a hug and a kiss. Then she shrouds me with her silky hair and perfumed warmth, and I fall in love all over again.

When I was little, my mother bathed herself in Opium—the perfume, not the drug. Rebecca smells not unlike this—with the cinnamon-drenched sweetness that I used to inhale while sitting on my mother's lap as my dad drove us toward our country home in the sun-filled family car, as I curled up to have a fairy tale read. It's a smell that reminds me of daydreams.

"So," Rebecca says as we settle into our chairs, as I order soda water for Kevin and me and she and Delia order another round, "are you ready for the big move?"

"What does being ready have to do with anything?" Kevin says, laughing.

"You have a point," she says. "No one is ever ready when they think they are, but when you aren't ready, the best things happen."

"A toast to the unprepared," says Delia, and I raise my glass.

The Dillards live a life of structured serendipity, of passionate pain and exquisite extremes, and I envy it. Rebecca has steered her rag-tag clan of three as they stumbled from divorces and trailer parks to professorships and suburban Victorians, always saved at the last minute by a marriage proposal, a fellowship grant, or a kind judgment in a court of law. They tease convention and tempt all kinds of fate, and they always land upright and ahead, laughing at the sleights-of-hand and their twists of fancy.

I want this family, his family—smoke, drinks, drugs, and all. Because it seems to me they (not unlike Russia) live life raw.

It is so easy to get caught up in the daily rush of my American life, of becoming an adult, of advancing in my career, carefully plotting it all out, that sometimes it all takes on a surreal haze, as if I am not experiencing it but watching it or participating in a scripted play. But if the Dillards are working off a script, at least it is a complex and multilayered one. A sharp, incisive David Mamet to my neurotic, insipid David Kelley. Their script has weight, and I like that because the scariest thing about life is that it is so damn mercurial. Nabokov wrote in his autobiography *Speak, Memory* that nature mandates that for us to enjoy life, we should not enjoy it too much. "Imagination, the supreme delight of the immortal and immature, should [according to Nature, not Nabokov] be limited." My reading of this is that if we refuse to live inside our mortal constraints—time being the biggest of them—we run a huge risk of going batty. But these constraints are of course tiresome and dull, and I find the ability to laugh at our standard relationship to time, mortality, morality, and so forth to be a very attractive trait, even if it is risky. I find the whole Dillard family very attractive, batty or not. They are fascinating, people like them. Almost too brilliant, too special for this world. Unchallenged by school but still Phi Beta Kappa. Black belted without effort. Awarded and accoladed while intoxicated. I am not sure how someone like that, how a whole family like that, can function alongside us mortals, but they do. I want to be immortal like them. And when Rebecca Dillard gives me a seal of approval and kisses me in that space between my mouth and my cheek, I feel for a moment that I will never die.

16

Moscow—In many ways the arrivals area at Moscow's international airport is just a larger clone of Pulkovo in St. Pete. An ominous toxicity hovers in the air, and the only working lights to speak of are the fluorescent variety: illuminated advertisements for hotels, casinos, and cell phone distributors. A few dusty bulbs hang from rusted chandeliers high above, but they are so dim that insects seem to avoid them. Instead, the flies gravitate to the scores of greasy, jet-lagged travelers who are dragging their cramped legs down the hard flight of stairs worn smooth by years of people passing through. They shuffle across the cold black floor, and without pause they push, roll, and tug their oversized carry-ons up to the kiosks that house the visa police. Gradually, order takes form: Russian citizens here, other CIS citizens there. Permanent residents here, foreign visitors there. You know you are in the foreigners' line because there are always a few suburban American couples with empty strollers primed to be filled with waiting post-Soviet orphans. Christian missionaries chat them up and offer authoritative advice about how to act when in the company of natives. "Always bring gifts," they say. "We find chewing gum to be popular."

Kevin rolls his eyes at the Mormon, in suit jacket and tie, to our left. His black plastic name tag with white engraved letters is partially obscured by the tattered strap of his brown leather carry-on. I can make out the white stenciled "Elder," though. Mormon elders are always so young looking. This one can't be a day older than twenty. It's funny, come to think of it. I think the missionaries are attracted to Russia for the same reason I am. But whereas I find that the chaos of the country liberates me, they want to liberate the country from the chaos. "The children are always very grateful," he is telling the pale, travel-worn couple supporting themselves on the handlebars of their Maclaren stroller. They nod vigorously, eager for any advice or guidance whatsoever.

"Let's go over there," Kevin says, pointing his stubbly chin to a line forming on our left. "I can't listen to this anymore."

"But that's for permanent residents."

"Well, I already am one and you will be soon. Come on." He arranges his knapsack on his back and marches us over. We cut to the front.

"Naglost'," someone mutters at our backs.

I like that word. To me the deep-rooted respect and deference for what Russians call *naglost'* is simultaneously the least and most attractive thing about them. The closest translation I can come up with is insolence, but insolence doesn't do the word or the characteristic justice. First of all, *insolence* is not a word one often hears in the American vernacular, whereas *naglost'* is about as common as, say, *ugly* or *rude.* It is so deeply part of the modern Russian cultural and linguistic fabric that if Russians had an equivalent of the SATs, the word wouldn't even rate a listing in the Princeton Review word list. Maybe it would crop up during an elementary school spelling bee. The point is, as Kevin pulls me to the front of the shorter but incorrect line, that people are put off enough to sneer but impressed enough to let us pass. The customs officials reward our chutzpah by reluctantly giving our documents stamps of approval.

"*Tri dnia.*" Three days, the tightly uniformed official tells me, squinting his eyes in what is presumably an attempt at a threatening glare. He waves my papers in front of his face for added effect, then passes my tattered blue passport back under the glass barricade between us. "You have three days to register with the local police," he repeats as he pushes through my customs forms and lavender tri-fold visa.

"Fuck that," says Kevin, as soon as the documents are in hand and we are walking away.

"Fuck what?" I say.

"Registration."

"Of course." His know-it-all airs bother me a bit, but I shove the bundle back into my jeans pocket anyway. "You aren't going to take my passport too?" I say to him snidely.

Kevin makes a mocking grimace, and I can't help musing that maybe there is a subtle connection between those women whose passports were stolen and me, with registration denied. Perhaps, I think, those women, the ones whose stories brought me here, the ones who answered innocent-sounding classified ads, only to wind up in basement brothels, maybe I am not so different from them. Not to say that my fate is anything like theirs, but there certainly is a sort of wing-and-a-prayer factor at play, both for them and for me. On some level I admire their enthusiastic responses to the opportunities those ads promised, even if they (the women, not the ads) were tremendously naive. And now, thinking about it, my heart breaks a bit at the tragic sense of trust that they had when they got on the plane. Think about it. How, when your trust is so dramatically abused, can you ever learn to trust anyone or anything again? And without trust, without the ability to jump on planes and fly off on wings and prayers, how can you go forward in life? Slowly, I guess. But who has patience for the methodical exploration of options? And when do options ever allow for the time such patience would require anyway? While you plod and ponder taking a job, hooking up with a man, eating a meal—that job gets filled, the man meets someone else, and the meal gets cold. That whole ethos that sees patience as a virtue and good things coming to those who wait—sometimes I think of it as a conspiracy thought up by usurpers. I have this image of beady-eyed people lurking in shadows, snickering softly as they wait to step in and grab things, people, thoughts.

I ponder a moment and then take the documents back out of my pocket.

"On second thought," I say, holding them up so Kevin knows what I am talking about. He raises his eyebrows and looks at me with an are-you-shitting-me sort of grimace. I put them away.

He's probably right, I think. And it's not like he is trying to keep me here secretly, against my will. Sometimes my imagination runs riot. I suppose it's just that a part of me wants to be official. Without registration, without a documented address, on some level I won't exist. Which is the idea, of course. I mean, registration is a tremendously complicated issue for expats in Moscow; it's a guaranteed conversation at any Western-style watering hole. Popular wisdom has it that you should never let the police know where you live. If you let them know, you are a sitting duck for a robbery. You might as well paint a sign: Rich Foreigner Lives Here. A lot of companies register their expatriate employees at false addresses or simply just to the office. It usually works. But since part of the deal with the network is that I am a local hire and not their bureaucratic responsibility, and because Kevin is still registered through his paper in St. Petersburg (according to his visa he isn't even cleared to travel in Moscow, although no one ever stopped him from doing so), we figure we can just wing it for awhile. Worst-case scenario: We will pay off whatever harassing officer or customs official questions our presence.

It doesn't take long.

It goes like this:

In theory free carts are supposed to be available for people to pile their luggage on once they drag their suitcases off the carousel. In practice, burly skycaps grab up all the available carts, leaving you no option but to pay exorbitant rates to have them transport your bags the thirty-odd feet to the final customs check. This service runs 50 rubles a bag, but we have no rubles. They won't take dollars. So Kevin goes to the ATM and tries to extract some Russian currency. He gets dollars. Then he stands in a line to exchange the dollars into rubles, while I stand with the skycap, who tells me that he will have to charge extra for the time we are taking up.

Finally, correct currency in hand, we pile our bags through the x-ray machine and approach the next petty uniformed tyrant. The blond baby-faced officer takes our customs forms and shakes his head.

"How much weigh?" he says in broken English, lifting his chin up and rolling his eyes downward.

"What?" Kevin looks like he is going to spit.

"You have exceed limit."

"But we aren't getting on the plane, we are getting off the plane."

"It is law."

"What law?" Kevin is blustery. I touch his shoulder in an attempt to calm his down. He ignores me.

"Tourist cannot bring so much," says the officer.

"We aren't tourists." Kevin grabs his papers and points out that he has a business visa. The officer points out that mine says "tourist."

"Fine, then it's all my stuff," says Kevin.

The officer says something about Kevin's not even being allowed in Moscow and starts filling out a form. "Thousand rubles," he says. Almost a hundred dollars.

Kevin puts his hand on top of the officer's to stop him from writing. With his other hand he offers a few hundred-ruble bills.

"In dollars," says the officer.

So I go and change the money back into our currency, at a loss of lord knows how much. We pay off our little bribe for half the "official" rate.

"We're going to go broke before we even get into the apartment," I say, pulling the bags off the x-ray machine. We pile them back on the cart (the skycap tells us that he will have to charge extra if he lifts them himself) and are finally cleared to move—straight into the arms of Kolya, our squat, beefy landlord, who wraps us in a quick but suffocating bear hug before we even emerge from the gate.

He releases us and tells us we have to hurry.

"Bystree, bystree," faster, faster, he says, pulling us and the cart through the crowds, away from the taxicab Mafia that has suddenly descended upon us. There are at least ten of them. Clearly, this is their turf, and they are very territorial. Having a friend help you out of the airport is not protocol. A few raised fists are angled in our direction, and we have no choice but to sprint with the overloaded, unbalanced cart out of the terminal, halfway down the airport access road to where Kolya parked his car.

"Bliad'," Kolya says about a thousand times over, spitting through the taunting jeers. *"Bliad'. Bliad'. Na Khui."* Cunts. Bitches. Go fuck yourself. Kolya curses with such passion, it sounds like a rant, like a rap song. He is still cursing as I crawl to the safety of the worn, foam-exposed backseat of the rusted red Lada. He and Kevin quickly load the car and tie the luggage onto the wooden wagon jury-rigged to the back. I grab the handle—half broken off—to close myself in.

"Podozhdi!" Wait! Kolya shouts before I can slam the door shut. He has to lift it off the frame entirely in order to snap it properly into place. "OK!" he says, thumbs up with pride once it is done. I curl up on the other side of the seat and pull the fake fur collar of my coat tightly around my neck.

They finish the loading, cover the wagon with a muddy black tarp, and we take off.

I think I am the only one whose heart is racing.

"Dzhenni," Kolya turns toward me as the car sputters onto the highway, instructing me to shout if anything falls off the wagon.

"OK," I say, smirking at the double entendre that he doesn't know he made. Thumbs up. He turns back around just in time to avoid a sideswipe with a large truck, a *gruzovik*, and keeps on chatting.

"Nu, Kevin," Kolya then says, emphasizing the second syllable of his name as *veen*, as in *vino*, the word for wine, and slaps Kevin's

back with a thick callused hand. "I already know it. I feel it in my gut." He pats the hard round belly bursting from beneath his jacket buttons. "You're like my fucking lost baby brother." Kolya speaks with the gruff accent of a workingman, the Moscow equivalent of a Staten Island twang. Expletives lace his diction like metaphors in a poem. His mouth hides his good intentions, but I think I know better. Kolya is the slightly annoying modern equivalent of Dostoevsky's simple man, of Tolstoy's peasant: the bumbling, unassuming, reluctant hero.

We drive through the Moscow streets as fast as the traffic allows, and from the benzene-fumed backseat, I wipe the icy fog off the window, trying to absorb the vibe of this city that is now mine. It is one of those crisp winter days when the sun is so bright that it seems to chill things instead of warm them. Stalled cars line the road, suggesting that the city is too frozen to penetrate. Moscow doesn't have the magic of St. Petersburg. I can't see any charm here. The roads are wide, seemingly infinite lanes across. The shoddy cement high-rises on the outskirts give way to the blocky five-story Khruschevki—the drab utilitarian dwellings that sprung up in the housing crisis of the 1950s. A feeling of dread washes over me. It was even worse than the dread I felt when I found that bottle. That was potential dread. But in the back of this fifteen-year-old dented Soviet car, passing through a city of millions, all unlike me, I am alone, and the dread is present, active. Kevin and Kolya are yammering on at a clip far too fast and colloquial for my comprehension. The fur-hatted masses milling on the sidewalks are too stereotypical to be real and, although I recognize the wide streets, the enormous but empty state-run stores, the signs, they all seem ethereal, as if I am driving through a dream and soon I will wake up in my Upper West Side bed, unable to remember the sequence of things that I have been experiencing for the past few months. Right now, I kind of want that to be the case.

The car plunges forward, tossing me up against the driver's seat. *"Priekhali!"* We've arrived! Kolya shouts as if we have won a race. *"Dorogaia moia, tvoi dvorets."* Your castle, my dear. His manic enthusiasm shakes me out of my anti-reverie, and the car's lack of shock absorption shakes me back into my seat. The rear entrance to our courtyard, the *dvor,* would have been better navigated with a 4 x 4. Instead, Kolya's tin can lurches in and out of dirt pits, spinning its wheels and spitting up the already disastrous lot. We plow around the gray brick building that houses the Moscow state prosecutor's office and finally land on the cracked asphalt directly in front of our building's door.

Kolya digs into his pants and pulls out two sets of oversized keys, which are so large and heavy that they look like toys.

"For you, Madame." He turns and hands me one, bows his head. "And for you, sir." He gives Kevin the other. Then he steps out and around to open the faulty car door, signals for me to get out, and attempts a regal curtsy. A man with a bulbous belly like that can't bend at the waist. He has to bend at the hip, sending his balance precariously forward. Imagine Tweedle Dee or Dum folded in half.

That is my greeting committee.

Kevin starts unloading the car, and Kolya, having regained his balance, walks me to the entrance door, explaining how to work the code. Eight. Nine. Zero, all at once. He presses the buttons with his stubby fingers until we hear a click. Then he does it again. And again.

"I think I got it," I say.

"Pokazhi," he says. Show me.

I press the code, wait for the click, and push open the heavy, dented steel door.

Jesus.

The air is saturated with the smell of fermenting cat piss.

I turn to open the next door, the one on the left that leads to our corridor, praying that the stench permeating the main entrance has not crossed the threshold. This wasn't something I noticed when we signed the lease.

"Kolya?" I call back into the yard. I sound nasal because I am holding my nose. "Is there a key for this one?"

"Net, net, net," he says and comes stomping back inside. *"Vot tak."* Just like this. He sticks his hand through the loose cardboard

117

flap on the door that covers what was once a window. He turns the lock from the other side.

"There's no key?"

"I'll get it for you soon," he says. "But you don't need it."

He pushes the door, but something prevents it from completing the swing. I suck in my stomach and slip sideways through the narrow opening. The cat smell is still here, hovering around the small hallway with a tangible physicality. I look down. Piss is spread out in front of the small, upside-down bathtub that is blocking the door, its rusted feet pointing into the air like a prostrate pig. Next to the tub is a grease-splattered gas stove.

I look at Kolya and furrow my brows.

"Those are the ancient remains," he explains. "Inside it is all new and beautiful. It is all coming along spectacularly."

"Coming along?" The renovations were supposed to be completed by now. I cross my arms tight around the waist of my coat and walk toward our door.

Apartment #2. Of the four apartments in our noxious corridor, it is the only one without a number on the post. A trail of sawdust and plaster specks spreads out over the ragged welcome mat. I step into the chalky mess and place the comically large key into the corresponding hole.

Kevin follows in behind us, kicking a few bags along the damp floor while balancing a few others on his back. "Wait," he says before I turn the lock. He dumps the bags over the rounded belly of the tub. "I need to carry you over the threshold."

I sigh. I smile. I jump into his arms.

He falls back a bit but catches his balance against the stove.

"Check this thing out," I say, holding the ridiculous key in front of his nose.

"Let's see if it works. Quick. I can't hold you much longer."

"Hey!" I pout and then turn the key in the lock. He kicks the door open with a hard bang from his red-laced Doc Marten boot and drops me on the other side.

"Hey!" I say again.

"Shit," he says and turns me around.

"Fuck."

There is not a lot else to say. New tub and stove aside, Kolya hasn't touched the place. The door to the bathroom is a bare wood skeleton frame. Exposed pipes and wires snake around the ceiling, and rolls of wallpaper are stuck half unspun against the walls. There is an empty space on the kitchen floor and an old hose where the washing machine once stood.

Kolya tosses the bags in after us and marches straight to the red enamel refrigerator. He pulls out a box of apricot juice and holds it up like a bottle of fine champagne. "Let's celebrate!" he says and begins to show off the beautiful new Italian stove, the electronic teapot, the slightly used but still functional Sony television set, as if he were giving a White House tour.

"I can't deal with this," I say and sit down on the bare bed across the room. I cradle my face in my hands, massaging my temples with my still-gloved forefingers as I wait to hear Kevin start berating Kolya.

But he doesn't.

Instead I hear him pouring out some juice and raising his glass for a toast.

"Do you want some?" he asks me.

I don't answer. My fingers work harder at my temple lobe, as if I can rub back the rage that is beginning to pump inside me.

"What's wrong?" Kevin says.

I raise my eyes but not my head.

"What?" he insists.

"*Chto? Chto proiskhodit?*" says Kolya. "*Nu, Dzhenni. Chto?*" What? What's wrong, Jenny, what?

Which is enough for me to slam a pillow against the wall.

It doesn't make a very large impact, the pillow, but it is enough to let loose a few feathers and some bile.

"Damn it, Kevin," I snap. "Aren't you planning to ask him what the hell happened to all the fucking repairs he promised to finish? Like where the fuck is the washing machine, and would it be too fucking much to ask for a fucking bathroom door when we are paying through our fucking asses for this dump?"

His eyes roll at the rag pile I have now become. He looks at Kolya, who is dumbfounded. Kolya might not speak a word of English but cannot possibly misunderstand my nondenominational rage.

"*Nu, chto,* Kevin? *Chto proiskhodit?*" What's up, Kevin? What's going on? Kolya says to Kevin with puppy dog eyes.

"I was getting to it," Kevin says to me through his yellow teeth. "I just wanted to ease into things."

It takes awhile. They are speaking too quickly for me to follow, but a box of apricot juice later Kevin ascertains that Kolya has blown all the repair money on the new Italian stove.

"We don't even cook," I say, tossing myself back onto the bed.

Another box of juice, and Kolya has convinced Kevin to fork over an additional month's rent so he can finish up the *remont*—the repairs—and buy us a new washing machine. He didn't think the old one was good enough for us.

"Well, now we won't have money to buy food, even if we did cook," I say.

"Cute," says Kevin.

"Can you please kick him out now?"

So Kevin explains to Kolya that I want to rest. Kolya says he will talk quietly. I give up and call Elena, who tells me that it will all be all right and promises to come by after work tomorrow to help me straighten up the place as best we can.

Hours later, when things have settled and our bed is made, when we finally close the door behind Kolya, Kevin gently places his hand on the back of my neck. I can feel the nicotine emanating from his skin.

"Anything interesting going on?" he asks. I am sitting on the edge of the bed, staring at the newscast on the black-and-white television.

I have to sit close, because every few minutes I need to adjust the rabbit ear antenna.

"I can't understand a word they're saying," I say, despondent.

He sits down next to me and translates for a while, softening my disposition.

"Yeltsin's delaying the vote on the new prime minister," he says. "Some coal mine director was assassinated in Siberia."

"I thought that's what they said."

"See, baby, your Russian is way better than you let on."

"Maybe," I say, not really sure. Maybe I understood the news because I got the context, not the content.

"Come on," he says, grabbing hold of my wrist.

I look at him. He doesn't look like a man who has just traveled a whole day, who has arrived at a disaster zone, whose fiancée is feeling defeated. He looks like a man ready to take on the night, energized, excited. Upright.

"Let's go somewhere."

I protest, claiming exhaustion, but he wins and so we do. He puts on his jacket (I still haven't taken mine off, four hours later) and we leave the apartment, past the tub and the stove and the urine, past the yard and into the subzero city.

The sun has long set, but the traffic and the billboards light the way for a sprint across the slushy four-lane street. I gather steam as we barrel breathlessly through the sky-high archway of the Krasnopresnyenskaya metro station and ride the two stops to Red Square for what Kevin says is our inaugural kiss. There in the postcard-perfect shadow of St. Basil's, in front of Lenin's tomb, everything starts to make sense again.

I no longer want to wake up from this dream. I can almost taste the immortality.

"Are you nervous about tomorrow?" Kevin asks sweetly as he takes my hand and leads me out of the Kremlin gate toward the McDonald's, up Tverskaya Street.

"Terrified."

"I'll be here for you." It's the right thing to say, but it's not really true.

"You'll be in St. Pete." He is due back at the paper for his final two weeks. I am due at the bureau first thing in the morning.

"A phone call away. Same time zone."

"Different world."

"Same world," he says, stopping to kiss me once again. He lights up an L&M.

"Can I have one?"

He gives me the one he is smoking and gets another out of the pack for himself.

"Welcome to Russia, baby," he says, cigarette bouncing from the side of his mouth.

17

Moscow—The network's Moscow bureau is located on the main floor of the Slavyanskaya Hotel. Originally an American-Soviet joint venture, the Slavyanskaya was one of the first establishments in Moscow equipped with enough Westernized touches to make folks from the States feel at home. Upscale boutiques and fancy restaurants line the entrance hall. It has a newsstand packed with English-language periodicals and a health club that features step aerobics and Cybex machines. But behind all that the culture is not apple pie American at all. In my poorer student days I occasionally took my friend Yulia there to indulge in a few frothy $5 cappuccinos and a pack of Camel Lights in the lobby cafe. Café Amadeus. Café Arm-and-a-Leg-Us in my college vernacular. From our posts at the marble-topped tables, Yulia and I watched Italian-suited, wedding-ringed businessmen sidle up to Barbie-doll beautiful call girls clad in Gucci and fur. After a few minutes of chitchat and giggles, they would totter away, arm in arm, toward the elevator banks. We watched processions of important-looking men with entourages of beefy guys walk through the marbled halls while other beefy guys stood in the shadows, whispering indecipherably into their wrists. Sometimes their hairy forefingers gently pushed at clear plastic earpieces, and, if we were lucky, we could spot a gun or two as they adjusted their sports jackets.

The accepted wisdom is that the Slavyanskaya is run by an unhappy partnership of Moscow's mayor, Yuri Luzhov, and some powerful Chechen mobsters. The American part of the deal was blown to bits a few years ago. Literally. The hotel was founded at the end of the glasnost era by a ballsy Oklahoma entrepreneur named Paul Tatum. Initially, the development went swimmingly well. George H. W. Bush and Mikhail Gorbachev blessed the place during their 1990 summit. Businessmen and tourists flocked to its restaurants and bars, celebrating and sealing deals over cabernet sauvignon and sirloins. Western media companies like my network, Reuters, and the BBC anchored the prestigious tenant list, glad to be located away from the drudgery of Russian life that they otherwise had to deal with every day. But when communism fell, the hotel ownership switched hands four times, ultimately landing in the hands of a Chechen contract killer named Umar Dzhabrilov. Not long after that, the hotel set up a casino where a nonprofit press center had been, meaty guys in black turtlenecks started to outnumber the well-dressed businessmen, and a 5.45-caliber Kalashnikov assault rifle was pointed at Paul Tatum's head. He died on November 3, 1996, lying in a pool of his own blood, which dripped down the stairs leading to the Kievsky Vokzal metro station underpass.

Now, a little more than a year and a half later, I am moving with the undulating masses through the once blood-splattered subway exit, up the hard stone steps, and out to the dirty, damp streets above. I separate from my fellow travelers as I cross the gate surrounding the Slavyanskaya and walk past the rows of black polished sedans and up to the covered, heated entrance where a white-gloved bellhop holds the door open for me. I have a bit of time to kill before I am due for my first day of work at the bureau, so I grab a copy of the *Moscow Times* from the concierge and make a beeline for a celebratory cup of cappuccino at Amadeus.

I can get used to this, I think, as the waiter places a porcelain plate filled with biscotti and a froth-filled mug on the marble table in front of me. I skim the paper's headlines, and, once confident that I haven't missed too much during our day of transit, I pull out the white sheet of paper on which I had printed my notes and lists of story ideas. With visions of duPont Awards and Emmys dancing in my head, I finish off the cappuccino and, heart racing, stand up to go to work.

The bureau itself is in a small office space behind a large glass door just past the main entrance, catercorner to a shop that sells gaudy gold statues and crystal chandeliers. A guard always paces in front of the store, a large semiautomatic slapping his thigh. At the bureau unarmed attendants sit behind the door and buzz people in or call for help when it's needed. Mostly, they pass time watching dubbed Mexican soap operas on the small black-and-white monitor balanced on the corner of the desk and gossip with the cleaning ladies.

I speak my name into the intercom.

The gaunt man with the blond crew cut who is sitting behind the desk buzzes me in without looking up from the television set.

He gestures, still not looking, for me to go to his left, which I do.

A dark-haired, darkly dressed young woman is sitting at the workstation just inside the bureau door. I explain who I am. She says her name is Mary and she is the only one here.

"Usually, no one arrives until about eleven," she says. "Welcome to a network news bureau, where nothing ever happens. Do you want some coffee?"

"No, thanks. I just had some."

"Join me for a smoke?" She tosses a black sheepskin jacket over her petite frame and I follow her back outside.

Mary tells me that she's been living in Moscow for almost five years. Originally from New Jersey, she came over upon completing a master's in Russian literature and never looked back. The television news business happened by default. When the White House (the Russian Parliament building) was under siege in 1993, the network desperately needed translators for all the clueless producers and correspondents they had flown in, and Mary desperately needed money. Five years later she is still here. Her official job is "desk editor"; she watches the wires, the news, and the phones, coordinates the crews, sets up satellite feeds, and has the honor of being the second-lowest person on the totem pole. She still has the interns to yell at. But this is her day job, and, generally speaking, it is completely undemanding. Mary's real passion is working as a liaison for American couples looking to adopt Russian orphans. Periodically, she takes a week or two off to help incoming couples navigate the corruption and bureaucracy and, they all hope, bring their dream child back to the States.

"I volunteered at an orphanage a few years ago," I tell her.

"So you care about this country?"

"I guess so," I say.

"Then you won't care for this job." She grinds out her cigarette butt against the dark marble wall of the hotel and goes back inside. I follow behind.

At around 11 o'clock people start trickling in. Mary gives me the lowdown on each, one by one, like a runway show. The research assistant is a Russian guy who was working as a nuclear physicist until he found that he could make more money doing grunt work for American journalists. There is a fiftysomething British camera operator who has seen too many wars and drunk too many drinks to forget them, the audio technician who really wants to be a tape editor, and an old BBC tape editor who recently married a Russian woman half his age. And there is the rotating pool of three desk editors, Mary included. A brand-spanking new correspondent, Douglas Marshall, and a new bureau chief, Sylvia Smith, are starting fresh with me.

We gather in Sylvia's office, piling onto the couch, squatting on the carpet.

To welcome the new team the network sent over one of its Emmy-laden veteran correspondents, a guy who was based in Moscow for a few years at about the time the cold war was ending. Mr. Emmy sits down in the large leather recliner opposite Sylvia's desk. She fawns on him, offering tea, then coffee. He declines, explaining that he outdid himself at breakfast. She laughs and they compare notes about overdone eggs and fresh-squeezed orange juice. The rest of us squirm, cramped in our seats.

We are waiting for Marshall. His new car hasn't been cleared by customs yet, so one of the bureau's drivers had to go pick him up.

"Where did they house him?" I ask no one in particular.

"Oh," the researcher-scientist says in a perfectly accented but disparaging tone, "the correspondent's apartment is in the CNN complex. On Kutuzovsky."

"Nice," I say. Kutuzovsky Prospect is a five-minute walk away, just past the new McDonald's.

"Where are you living?" Mary asks me.

"Next to the zoo, on Krasnya Presnya"

"No, shit."

She says we are neighbors, that she lives on the other side of the prosecutor's office.

"Oh, I think I know where that is," says Sylvia. "I just bought some kitty litter at that supermarket across the street."

"The Su-pier Mark-yet," I say, mimicking the large transliterated Cyrillic sign I noticed this morning.

"Exactly."

We are all gregarious. On good behavior.

"No more universams anymore, huh?" laughs Mr. Emmy, misusing the old Soviet word for large department stores. He leans over and taps me lightly on my stocking-covered knee.

"Oh, it's a regular Wal-Mart I've got on my block, honey," I say, exaggeratedly batting my eyelashes. He laughs again, and I relax into the couch. We banter some more. Mr. Emmy asks about my ring. I say I am engaged. They all say they know Kevin's name from his bylines.

"I'll bet he's got some good connections," says Sylvia.

"His connections are all mine," I say, emphasizing the *all*. I smile.

"Who's got the connections?" The question resonates around the room, but it emanates from the chisel-chinned man walking in the door. His voice has that deep broadcast timbre, and his head has that perfect broadcast hair, with just enough gray to garner respect. "Hello, everybody," he says to nobody, pale blue eyes scanning the room.

"Doug!" Sylvia jumps up. "We were beginning to get worried."

He ignores her and takes the seat that the researcher has vacated for him.

"This is Douglas Marshall," Sylvia says, even though we already know. She points her finger at each of us, reciting fractured but embellished biographies as she circles the group. When the greetings subside, she runs through a well-practiced monologue about her vision for the bureau and the network's enthusiasm for all the fresh blood.

We talk story ideas. I list mine (and Kevin's). Mr. Emmy picks at his fingernails.

"These are great ideas, Jen." He says this without one drop of enthusiasm.

"But?"

"But they will never fly with New York."

"Oh, come on," says Marshall, coming to my rescue. "Those are fabulous ideas. I love the one about the off-shore money in Cyprus. What elements do you have for that?"

"Look," says Mr. Emmy before I can answer. "These are important and interesting stories but they aren't clichés. As much as I hate to say it, after almost twenty-five years at the networks, I have learned the hard way that our job is to perpetuate the clichés."

I am silent.

"Don't tell anyone I ever said that," he adds with a nervous laugh.

It didn't actually put me off, though, his comment. I suppose it should have, but I have to believe that clichés serve some purpose in this world, seeing as they're so abundant, seeing as I am as guilty as the next person of using them time and again. At my new perch as a prestigious network producer, I want to believe that the clichés we are asked to report are innocent, sweet coatings that ease the deliverance of whatever harsh reality we will be sharing with the 9.7 million homes that tune in to our particular broadcast airwave. And, anyway, I quickly discover that clichés are the least of the problem. In the year before my arrival at this network, its top-rated evening news program aired only two full-length features produced out of Moscow. In the first couple of weeks at my job, I have literally nothing to do but practice my Russian, compose lengthy e-mails to my friends back home, and make free long-distance calls to Kevin while he finishes his stint in St. Pete.

"Hey," I say into the slick black Lucent headset.

"Hey," he says into his bulbous yellow receiver as the clicking and clacking subsides.

"Everything in order up there?"

"Well, Kesha wasn't shy to express his displeasure at my absence."

"You've been back for days."

"Tell that to Kesha."

We banter about the cat's incontinence, about the miserable weather, about my struggle to find drinkable coffee beyond the hotel. We talk about the musical chairs being played in the Kremlin, the eminent collapse of the nation, and all the deep-pocketed Rasputins waiting in the wings. We laugh about my lack of work at the network. Kevin begs me to let him do an exposé about the correspondent's cliché comment and I beg him not to. I beg him to quit his job up there early and come be with me. He begs me to wait.

"Aren't you having fun hanging with Yulia?" My old friend Yulia has been sleeping next to me in place of Kevin. I was afraid to be alone at night, and she was happy not to sleep at her parents' over-populated two-room apartment, so she is living with me for the time being. Yulia, whom I met at a nightclub almost ten years ago, when we were nineteen.

"I didn't move here to sleep with Yulia," I say.

And when Kevin finally does come down to share our premarital bed, two weeks later than his originally scheduled appearance, it is with heavy reluctance and a strong splash of remorse.

The night before he gets on the plane, he tells me that I am not sensitive enough about how hard it is for him to uproot himself from St. Petersburg, his adopted home.

"At least you know how to negotiate the price of an apple," I say. "I can't even do that." I say I am scared. I feel isolated.

"You think you are the only one making a sacrifice?" he says, not in a nice way. He tells me I am selfish to think that I am the only one who gave up a lot for this adventure. In fact, he says, considering that I was a bit bored with my life in New York, this transition is perhaps an even greater sacrifice for him.

"That is so unfair," I say. So when he arrives the next day, he brings along a reminder of the disparity.

I open door and he hands me a damp duffel bag.

"What's this?" I say, although I recognized the smell immediately. Kevin brought along Kesha, and apparently Kesha had an episode or two of aggressive incontinence during transit.

"Jesus!" I hand the bag back, turning my head to breathe. "I thought we were going to let Ivan settle in first?" I wanted my cat to be the alpha cat, but he is still in New York. I've been planning to send for him when things settle.

"I changed my mind." He unzips the bag. A small scared little creature pops out. There is a harness made out of torn rags tied around his torso.

Kesha is shaking, and I soften immediately. I am charmed that Kevin can't bear to leave his pet in the care of someone else, charmed at his pathetic kitty transport device, charmed by the mottled little fool of a cat who let him put it on.

"He sprayed all over me. And all over the passenger next to me," says Kevin as he struggles to untie the knots. "I had to put him in this sack to keep the asshole from killing both of us."

I laugh and kiss his cheek and Kesha's head, and then I throw them and all their belongings into the shower. Kevin pulls me in for the rinse. A few minutes later we emerge, scratched, bleeding, wet. We scramble over to the bed and curl up under the crisp down duvet. Kesha nibbles at my ears while Kevin nibbles elsewhere. And, in the interest of perpetuating clichés, I will just say that at that moment, curled up in intimate pretzels and licking each other's wounds, I think for a moment that this might be the calm before the storm.

"What?" he says, noticing my attention has slipped.

"Nothing," I say. I say nothing.

18

MOSCOW—In the course of my career I have had a history of near hits and frustrating misses. I missed the '91 coup by eight hours. The tanks rolled down Svetnoy Boulevard as my plane slowed to a halt on the tarmac at JFK. I found out what was going on when my father turned on the radio in our Toyota minivan as it was heading down the Van Wyck Expressway. "I can't believe I'm not there," I cried as the announcer described the events in Red Square. "I am so glad you are not there," cried my mother. Three years after that, I missed Yeltsin's assault on the White House by a little over a month. In domestic news my job at MSNBC started two days after TWA Flight 800 plummeted into the sea. But Kevin, he is a magnet. When he finally moves down from St. Petersburg into our Moscow hovel, the news really begins to break. Nuclear leaks, border skirmishes, and SALT treaties are the least of it. The big news is the beginning of the end of the Yeltsin administration. Three contentious rounds at the Russian parliament, the Duma, and thirty-four-year-old Sergei Kiriyenko is named prime minister. The West is once again hailing a new breed of adolescent reformers and presumed visionaries, the next great hopes. No matter that highways of evidence suggest that these young guns are just as corrupt and sold-out as the gray suits before them. The political game of musical prime ministers is running almost daily on page one of the *New York Times,* thereby deeming the story important enough to report on the evening news. The minute-long wire-spun packages aren't duPont Award worthy and certainly require no flak jackets, but they keep me busy. They keep both of us busy, adrenaline flushed, exhausted.

And so, when the phone rings early one Saturday morning, our first Saturday without work, I let it ring out. I am lying in bed, waiting for Kevin to return from a cigarette run. Kesha has claimed a light beam on the pillow next to me and I roll over to steal his spot. Unfazed, the cat lurks back, draping his mangy self across the side of my waist. We share the sun. I reach out, scratch his head. This is the kind of morning I have been longing for. Gentle, warm, and amber hued. Soon Kevin will be home, and he will bring coffee to me in bed. We will sip and giggle and, once caffeinated enough to prevent the otherwise inevitable headache, we will fall back onto the downy pillows and tangle around each other again and again.

Kevin's cell phone rings. It could be work related.

"Shit." I push Kesha aside. Five of my naked footsteps slap across the cold cement floor. "Alo?" I say, speaking no language in particular.

"Is Kevin there?" asks a beautifully accented female voice. I say he is not.

"It's Anastasia." Kevin's ex. The mother of the child that people say looks a bit like him, although we would never assume . . .

"Hello," I say, more as a question than a greeting.

"I couldn't get through on your other line." Not that I asked.

"I was asleep."

Anastasia doesn't apologize. Ahhnastasia, not Ann-astasia. "So, is Kevin there?" She says his name with propriety, as if she were talking about her son, brother, or husband. Keeh-vhin, not Kevin. As if she were British. Or he were. "There is a breaking story he might be interested in."

"Really?" I say, interested. "What's going on?"

She doesn't answer my question. "Just tell him to check his e-mail," she says and hangs up.

I think about checking it myself but instead take the floral sheet that covers the sofa, wrap it around myself, and call my office.

On weekends the network bureaus are usually staffed by eager young college graduates. They sit and watch the news, read the papers, cull through the wires, and alert New York if anything of importance happens. Back in 1991, when the coup broke out, no one was at this particular bureau, and no one at the network was aware of the situation for hours. Now, when news breaks, there is, in theory, someone in place to catch it.

The phone rings five times before anyone picks up. When the most recent of the recent college graduates answers, he says he has no idea about any breaking stories.

"Read me the headlines from the TASS wire," I tell him.

I can hear him sitting down at the terminal: "'Albright expected to make stopover in Yekaterinburg,'" he begins. "'Russian Experts Amend Their Part of Work on ISS. Fate of Russian Envoy Kidnapped in Chechnya Unknown. Japanese Lawmakers Start Uzbekistan Tour. May Day Holiday in Moscow Passed Calmly. U.S. National Attacked by Neo-Nazis in Moscow.'"

"Wait. What was that?"

"U.S. National Attacked by Neo-Nazis in Moscow."

"Oh, my God. Read me the text."

He is clicking around the keyboard, perhaps scrolling down the screen, trying to figure out how to open the full document.

"Well?" I say.

"OK, here it is. 'A U.S. national of African origin was beaten up by a gang of neo-Nazis Saturday in a park in western Moscow, the U.S. embassy here said. An embassy spokesman, John Hanson, said the victim, whom he did not name, was shopping in the area around the Fili Park when the skinheads pounced.'"

"Get Hanson's number," I say. "It should be in the database."

"Now?"

"No. Finish reading."

"'He said the victim was slightly injured and received treatment. In a communiqué, the embassy urged U.S. citizens, particularly those of African or Asian origin, to take care in areas such as Fili where skinheads are known to be active.'"

"Jesus, this must have happened hours ago." Too much detail for a breaking story.

"Should I go on?"

I don't answer, so he does.

"'The embassy issued a similar warning two weeks ago following an attack by twenty skinheads on two women of Asian origin. Although there are reports of rising violence against foreigners, Russian authorities say they are not told of specific attacks.'"

"Is that all?"

"Yes."

"Transfer me to Doug's cell."

"What, you think that's a story?"

"Of course it's a story." The bitchiness of my own tone gives me a charge. "Just transfer me. And get Hanson's number. And call Sylvia."

Of course it's a story. All the ingredients are there. An American is the central character. The foreign land is a violent place. Good and evil are clearly defined. And anything with the word *Nazi* in the title is a guaranteed purchase by the home office. It is all part of the policy of making the audience feel safe. The world is a bad, bad place, but if you watch our newscast, you will know how, and from whom, to protect yourself. Of course these rules apply regardless of what the dateline is. The thing is that at home, at least the viewers have a chance of perspective. Militias might be terrorizing entire counties of Texas, but Uncle Sidney's partner's wife has family out there and she says things are fine in Dallas. She is able to go shopping at Neiman's with no problem. No problem at all. When the only feature-length stories that come out of Russia are about turmoil, crime, and violence, well, that's all the public knows. But it makes such a good story. Good stories make good careers.

"Great job, Jennifer," Doug tells me when I get him on the line.

"Can you turn something around for this evening?" asks the executive producer of the weekend news.

"Meet me in Fili Park," I tell the camera operator.

I am fully dressed and ready to go when I hear Kevin jingle his keys in the door. I run to open it for him.

"OhmygodIamsogladyouarehere!" I say before he crosses the threshold.

He leans forward for a kiss, but I push him back. Breathless, I tell him about the attack, that it is for the evenings news. My first full-length package. "What do you think? I am meeting the cameraman at Fili. Is that where I should start?"

"Shit," he grins in his impish, slightly devilish way, "start with me."

Of course. He has contacts. He has already done numerous stories about neo-Nazi groups. Of course he knows where we could find some skinheads willing to go on camera, who will have the best file footage if we don't have enough in the office. He knows everything. By the time I walk into the bureau, freshly kissed and peacock proud, I am a golden girl, and Kevin has half-written the article that his *Newsday* boss excitedly commissioned. And by the time I return to the apartment, it is midnight and I am high on the adrenaline of the day's shoot, the seconds-to-air feed of the tape, the sense that I have arrived.

"Hey!" I say, slamming the door behind me, tossing off my leather jacket, and waltzing into our studio. "You should have seen it. It was just like that scene in *Broadcast News* when Joan Cusack is running to get the tape to Holly Hunter and—"

"Why didn't you tell me Anastasia called?"

He is sitting at the kitchen table, laptop open, cigarette burning in the ashtray at its side. Not hello. Not how are you. The first thing my fiancé says to me after my first triumph at work, our triumph, really, is "why didn't you tell me Anastasia called?"

I stub out his cigarette and give him what I think to be a cute but disapproving look. He isn't supposed to smoke in the apartment.

"Anastasia called, right?" he says. He starts to reach for a fresh cigarette but stops, arm stretched out, hovering over the pack, his tired eyes locked on mine. Like a threat.

"Sorry. I thought I told you. She just wanted to let you know about the Nazi thing."

He curls his lip slightly, shakes his head no.

"She said she was sending you an e-mail about some breaking news."

"She sent me an e-mail. It had nothing to do with the neo-Nazi thing."

"There was no other big story today. Was there?" I would think I would have heard about it.

He says he has to finish his article for *Newsday,* ignoring my question. I want to apologize about not relaying the message, but he turns to face the computer.

I suppose this is what most marriages are like. The kinds of unions that probably exist in those households that ultimately contribute to the 50 percent failure rate. Every movement is like an angry dance, choreographed to send a message. Back in bed, I jerk the quilt high over my head and roll to my side, away from him.

"Could you keep it down?" I mutter from under the covers. "I can't sleep with all your banging."

Kevin ignores me and continues to pound at the keyboard, the incessant tap-tap-tapping of the keys a not-so-slow form of torture. Finally, there is a pause. I sit straight up, knocking a few pillows to the floor.

"Wasn't your deadline at midnight?" I say.

He ignores me and begins typing harder.

On my laptop.

I get up and go back to the bathroom.

"Planning to sleep in the bathtub?" he calls after me in a dry, spiteful tone.

"I would if we had a door," I spit back through the skeletal frame. That is his responsibility, getting on Kolya's back about the missing glass, the absent knob.

I putter about the bathroom, washing my face, searching my

reflection for a resolution, a pimple to pop. I don't find any and leave the bathroom to crawl back into bed.

"You left the light on," he says.

"So?" I say, once again covering myself.

Silence.

Then typing.

"Jesus," I mutter and roll fetal-tight.

It seems like his writing is getting louder, more violent, if that is possible.

I sit up again. A new tactic. "Do you like how the article is coming along?" I ask. Soft, gentle voice. I am a supportive spouse.

Kevin stops again. He looks at me across the room. It is an odd look, one that is surprisingly blank for someone who was so hostile just a moment ago. Our eyes catch awkwardly and I have to avert mine.

I do not know him.

He doesn't answer, so I slowly raise my eyebrows in inquisitive fashion.

He says it has to be perfect, to knock the editors off their asses.

I say they might be even more impressed if he could make deadline. I know immediately that it isn't a nice thing to say. "Sorry, that didn't come out right."

"Fuck you," he says in a manner not so hostile as worn.

"I just want you to do well, but I am too tired and grumpy to express it in a nice way," I say, sort of lying, sort of telling the truth.

"It's not like some fucking crash-and-burn television package, you know." This is definitely not a nice thing to say.

"Excuse me?" My eyebrows have dropped and I am now squinting in disbelief.

"Just because you whipped up some sensational piece of shit, using my contacts, I should add, and those network pricks are now doing some celebratory circle jerk about it, doesn't give you the right to be my fucking judge and jury." He sits up straight, faces me square on.

"I have no fucking idea what you are talking about, Kevin."

"Yes, you do."

"Hey, I am sorry if you are jealous because I had a good day at work. My first good day yet, I might add. You might consider being happy about it for me." I pause for a second. "Don't take your deadline pressure out on me. You fucked that up, not me."

"If I hadn't spent so much time spelling out all the details to you, giving you all the fucking information, there would be no pressure."

"Oh, fuck you. I gave you as many contacts as you gave me and you know it." It's true. Some of the information he gave me was phenomenal, but there were other things, numbers for government officials, people at our embassy, that I got for him. "And, apparently, if it weren't for me, you wouldn't have even known there was a goddamn story to write."

"Whatever." He starts typing again.

"Christ." I throw myself back under the blankets.

I can hear him light up again. I can smell the sulfur from the match. He types for a few more minutes and then walks over to the bed.

"I'm sorry," he says to the back of my head. I turn over to face him. He caresses my cheek with a smoky hand. "I'm done now."

This is what I do. This is what I have always done. Give me a little affection and I forgive. Give me a lot of affection, I forget.

"I'm sorry too," I say. For what I do not know.

He kisses me with that ashtray mouth, tickling me with forty-eight-hour stubble. "I'll go brush my teeth," he says. "Wait for me."

"You know I will."

Moments later I feel cool mint blowing over my face. He hovers over me, lips not touching me, and slowly moves down. His fingers trace the elastic of my underwear, down from my hip, across my groin. He meets no resistance as he gently reaches beneath and inside.

"Are we OK?" I ask after ecstasy subsides into somnambulance.

"I adore you," he says. He kisses my forehead and moves over to dream.

I, on the other hand, do not. Cannot. I lie still, replaying in my mind the course of the day, wondering where my misstep lay. I didn't give him a message, but he got the story. We got the story.

A snore, some passed gas. He is sound asleep. I get out of bed, pad across the dark room, the cold floor, open the laptop. The LCD screen immediately illuminates my face, which, I imagine, isn't looking its best. Cheeks raw from stubble burn, eyes red from causes various and sundry. The image on the screen comes into focus as the computer creaks, waking from its own sleep cycle, opening up to an unsent e-mail. The spell check has just been completed, but Kevin forgot to check off the answer to that simple question: "Send now?"

I sit down on the cracked red vinyl that pads the steel chair, the torn edges of the hard synthetic fabric digging into my skin. I move the cursor across the screen and check "no."

TO: Josh.Smith@condesnast.com
FROM: JenandKevin@orc.ru
DATE: May 2, 1998
SUBJECT: Snap off panties

Hey bro. We've more or less completed the move to Moscow. I am now working as the bureau chief for Newsday, and am waiting to hear about a position with AP that looks promising. The *Newsday* thing sounds impressive but is really hilariously easy. They can't be bothered with the daily—or even monthly—ins and outs of the Byzantine Kremlin scene and only really give a shit about the "news" if it concerns Americans, like a marine guard from the American embassy who got his ass kicked by a bunch of skinheads today. But the new prime minister appointing a new government? Forget it. Too complicated. Otherwise, the rest is writing longish features for them and the more they make this place sound like Mars the more they like them. The rules, as far as I can discern them, are simple: the weather must always suck and preferably be snowy, though that is pushing the bounds of plausibility in the end of April, so the reader, for the time being, will simply have to settle for "gray"; old people preferably will appear somewhere in each file, hocking some heirloom or other on a street corner to compensate for their pathetic pensions—their wrinkled faces, too, will hopefully be described as "creased by years of communist despair"; the concept of "reform" will always be denoted as "slow" or "painful"—but NEVER as the far more accurate "non-existent." But this former clause is assuming you've gotten into politics at all, which, as I said, are preferably ignored unless they can be described as "Byzantine." Having accomplished that usage, the rest of the story should remain completely unexplained. Bearing these things in mind, everything else is fair game.

In other news, your pal at *GQ* rejected the piece on sex-slave trafficking pretty much outright because something or other on something remotely similar had appeared in the magazine recently, but he suggested we "brainstorm" over other ideas out of Moscow. I may be grasping at some pretty tiny crumbs of encouragement, but I think I'll write him back, kissing his butt, and pitch a couple of ideas.

Anyway, I'm beat, but I hope all is well back there. Write soon and let us know. Take care, and more about snap-off panties later.

K

This is odd. This is odd. This is what he was writing. This is what kept him up, caused our fight. It is troubling, extremely troubling, that this missive to one of his closest friends reveals none of the insecurity and fear I know he feels about the new job, the new city, the new responsibilities. And it is absolutely horrifying that he talks about snap-off panties. I don't mind sharing the ins and outs of my sexual antics with intimate interested parties, and I don't mind my lover's kissing and telling. But there is a big problem here. I don't own any snap-off panties. And this isn't some delirious locker-room fantasy, because as I drill deeper into our "sent mail" folder, I find this:

TO: Anastasiab@spbpress.ru
FROM: JenandKevin@orc.ru
DATE: May 2, 1998
SUBJECT: missing you
Darling,
I am so sorry for my tardy response. Your prose, however, was steamy enough to keep me, well, punctual for a long time to come. Yes, my

dear, my lady of lingerie and slippery satin, of course I am missing you. I am missing you always. Please don't hold it against Jen, though. She is the innocent here. And although I do hope to avoid the romantic gymnastics that seem to be all the rage among you married folks up in St. Pete, don't think I won't be sinning with you in my heart. It would take way more than a marriage to get images of you, with your fabulous ass and those snap-off panties, out of my mind. And please, please stop worrying. You are all over-reacting. Everything is under control.

A long, slow virtual lick between your thighs, Kevin

I think sometimes when something really terrible happens, it can cause such an unfamiliar emotional response that instead of feeling anything, you kind of go into shock. That is what happens to me. Instead of crying or screaming or throwing things, all I can do is intellectualize them. I think to myself that I don't know what is worse, that he wrote this or that he forgot to delete it. I think about how I really need to get some sleep. I think about Anastasia.

Kevin once said that Anastasia looks like me. That I look like her. We look like the same person and I hate her.

I can't find the e-mail, the one she had called about. I guess Kevin at least had the foresight to delete that. But I don't delete anything. I leave the laptop open, prone. And open and prone, I lie on the bed, next to him, wishing on some level that I were a corpse or that he was. Maybe on some level we both are.

I lie there through the night, wanting badly to release the stone-hard tears stuck in my throat, in my stomach. But I can't. This is what it feels like to be murdered, I think, as I lie silently. I am unable to cry, unable to scream. I am completely alone, even if we are lying together.

In the morning Kevin brings me coffee in bed. I drink it, but I don't speak to him. And, a little later, when I emerge freshly showered, I know that he has discovered the open e-mail, which is illuminated by the desk light that I had directed at it, like in an interrogation. I know he doesn't know for sure if I have or have not read it, but he is sitting there, at the kitchen table, staring gape-jawed at the screen. Silently staring. Mute.

"I am going to Elena's," I say, zipping up my boots, the tall black ones that make me feel solid, supported. "Don't forget to call Anastasia back if you haven't already." For a moment I consider lashing into him, saying something snide about snap-offs, but my passivity seems somehow more powerful.

He looks at me, looks scared at me. "Can I come?" he says, meekly.

"No. I need some girl time." I push open our heavy steel door and descend into the metro for the fifteen-minute ride to Rechnoi Vokzal.

I find solace in the subway. It's like New York. It's like home. People, stoic and silent. The silence of scores of people sharing a ride. We cautiously eye one another, careful not to get caught. I know, in Moscow, that I stand out, that I look different. I like it. I like this sense of not being placeable. I know that I don't look like what they think an American should look like, and I know I dress too well, too Western, to be Georgian, Caucasian, Azerbaijani, to be a refugee. I imagine that they think I am from Spain, from France. I enjoy this thought, this thought that I am not me. For fifteen minutes I am not me.

Out on the street again I stop to buy a few bananas and a loaf of bread from a sidewalk vendor, a leather-faced woman of indiscernible age. I pretend I don't speak any Russian at all, miming at the fruit displayed on the stained kitchen cloth that was laid carefully, crease-free, on the ground. A little girl stands at her side, her dress in tatters, her plastic doll naked, a finger in her nose. Her own nose, not the doll's.

I pay for the fruit, and the woman thanks me and I nod, mute, and deliberately forget to collect the change. The little girl calls after me to let me know, to tell me they owe me money. I continue to pretend I don't understand her and walk on.

At the apartment on Festivalnaya Ulitsa, Elena greets me as if she has been expecting me, as if she is a psychic, a sage. And I don't feel I need to explain anything, not really. It's obvious. She kisses my cheeks, right, then left, and I kiss hers and hand her the bananas. She laughs, gesturing to a bunch she says she just bought an hour before.

From the woman with the dirty girl, I ask? No, she says, from the man with no teeth. We giggle and I offer to bake banana muffins, because it is the one recipe I know.

We speak in Russian. We always speak in Russian, although I am not really sure why. Habit, I guess. The truth is, English trips along her tongue much more gracefully than Slavic does mine, although I doubt she would ever admit it. She would laugh and say I am too humble, too kind. She would be wrong.

So she says to me, in Russian, as she stirs two cups of flour into an aluminum mixing bowl, "men drink and men lie. That's life, really." She looks up as if to make sure Mikhail, who is in the other room playing on the computer with Dima, can't hear. And I laugh and say, in broken Russian, "He wasn't drinking, just lying and cheating. Thinking about cheating." Actually, I say "thinking cheating"; I drop the preposition and misconjugate the verb. But she gets it and says, "Well, then you have it better than most women." I try to explain how lying isn't really an acceptable option, and she tries to explain what she sees as the big difference in expectations between Russian and American women when it comes to their men, and I say that maybe American women have expectations that are too high after all, and we laugh and drink tea and bake muffins and bitch about men. Just like I do with my American girlfriends. It feels good.

And then she says to me, in English, "Do you regret this?"

"This what?" I say, happy to revert to my native tongue.

"You know. Kevin. Coming in Russia." OK, her English isn't perfect. But I don't really know what to say, in any language. I get up to check the oven.

I have been asked many times what my biggest regrets are. I mean, even before all this. Before Russia, before Kevin. It's just one of those things people ask. I find it a fascinating question. Not because I ever have an answer but because I never do. Not really. To me, the idea that someone might actually sit around compiling such a list or think of anything in such terms is certainly provocative, but I am not sure it is constructive. It might be cathartic or somehow educational; maybe such a practice is encouraged in certain schools of psychological thought. But think of all those time-travel films in which the slightest change of the past dramatically affects the present. They make a point. So it seems to me that if you like your current life at all, if you like the general trajectory in which you feel you are moving, then regret is a hypocritical emotion. And besides, the minute you might learn something from a so-called regrettable action or feel some positive development thrust forward because of it, it isn't really regrettable any longer, is it? Sad, sorrowful, even painful, perhaps. But regrettable?

There is not one moment of time with Kevin that I regret, not even after I found that bottle. I certainly don't regret making the decision to follow my gut, even though it is becoming patently clear that my gut is very unreliable. And while I do have very deep concerns about reporting to my friends and family back home that I am heading down what I know they will see as a potentially turbulent path, regret just isn't the proper descriptive for what I am feeling. Ashamed, perhaps. Which is why I am talking to Elena, not to them. But in some ways, somehow, I feel proud. I mean, I feel a little distress for the fear, anger, and pain that I know they would experience if they knew my fiancé has a cheating heart, that I caught him drinking back in March, yes. I know they would tell me to leave him, to just pack up and go. But I can't. I wouldn't know where to go. Back to New York, with no job, no place to live, no love? No. All relationships have obstacles, and I cannot say nothing positive will evolve even from this. And, besides, it got me here, didn't it? I am a network news producer in a foreign bureau. And I am engaged. So, if there is any overriding sentiment that I am feeling right now, sitting here, baking and giggling with my girlfriend, it is that this will all pass. Yes, I know things are bad, but they are workable. That is, if we can work through it, we will be stronger for it. Our marriage will be stronger. I mean, did you see the look on his face when I left? He wants this to work too. He is terrified at the thought of us failing. And that is good, because if we can face these fears—oh, here are the clichés again (but they work! they have purpose!), we can conquer them.

We call Kevin and invite him to come join us, with Mikhail and Dima, for some fresh-baked muffins and tea, although the muffins are cold by the time he arrives.

"It's already stale," he says when he takes a bite.

"Then don't have any," I say and reach to remove the plate from in front of him. He grabs my hand to stop me and then quickly eats the whole thing, scattering crumbs across the wooden table. When he goes to the balcony to smoke a cigarette, I brush them away.

19

ST. PETERSBURG—The tinny disco beat is pulsing out of the passing car, its shell too thin to keep the sounds to the driver, but the muffler dead enough to drown the vocals before they escape into the city. On the sidewalk we hear only the bass, an electronic pulsation that compels us to tick and torque our torsos in a manner reminiscent of those characters on *Saturday Night Live,* the ones who go to discos and slam into women under the strobes. Suddenly, the car lurches forward and the vibrations dissipate down the street, creating a vacuum of sound in their wake. Like when a record skips. Like when, in a sitcom, the actor breaks out of character and addresses the camera directly. Silence exists for a second, suggesting a passing of time, a change in scene.

It is late spring, and the weather in St. Petersburg has started to soften. March's mud-covered streets have dried out; the rings of dirt left by evaporating streams hint at the summer dust to come. The sun starts to set at times more appropriate to our biological clocks, and the shadows on the sidewalks are supple. This is the time of year when the expat community's softball league gears up, beer in hand, hats on heads, English in the air. Kevin and I have come up from

Moscow to attend to a few final packing details, say a few more goodbyes, and cheer the inaugural pitch.

"Buy me some peanuts and Crackerjacks!" sings a stringy guy as he sits down next to me on the splintered wood bleacher bench. He sings loudly, almost shouting, "I don't care if I never come back!" and puts one foot up on the bench to retie his ratty red Converse All-Stars, consequently getting dried-up dark, crusty flakes all over the place.

"Sorry, 'bout that, dude," he says. To me.

"The mud or your singing?"

"Both."

I laugh. "Don't worry about it," I say. "You're kind of transporting me home."

"This here dirt is Russian dirt." He brushes some to the ground. "The *Rodina*." The Motherland. He says this, mimicking the accent of a Texas rancher.

I laugh again. "I meant the chant."

"I sing so bad you need to escape back to the States, huh?"

"No, no. It's nice. Just feeling a bit homesick, you know?" If he only knew.

"You must be Jen?" His sneakers are now tied and placed squarely on the ground in front of him. Feet set shoulder-width apart, hands on knees—the body language of an American man.

"Yes," I say, thinking it odd that nostalgia should be my give-away. "Are you someone I should know of?"

"You bet." He tips the tattered Mets cap on his head. A few deviant strands of dirty blond hair fall forward from under the brim, and he looks at me as if I am supposed to take a stab at guessing.

I furrow my brows, twirl my ponytail for effect.

"Luke," he says, extending his hand. "Your fiancé's guardian angel."

"I thought that was supposed to be me," I say but shake his hand anyway.

Luke doesn't say anything. He just motions his head at the field, gets up, and runs toward it.

I have heard of Luke. I've even spoken to him on the phone, but he isn't what I expected. I expected a bookish nerdy administrator type, mostly because I know he administers an exchange program. But the guy here seems more like a California surfer. He runs past Kevin, hands hitting a high five, and takes his place in the outfield, takes his place among all Kevin's friends, among the people Kevin has been so reluctant to leave, to give up in order to be with me.

I like them, his friends. And I like him with them. With them he is joyous, serene. With them he sings songs from left field; he shares gloves and cheers people to base.

When, back at the start, my father asked me whether Kevin was the kind of person who lived abroad because he wanted to or because he had to, I laughed dismissively, not really understanding the question. But, now, sitting on the bleachers, observing his group of friends, this makeshift family, I finally understand. These are, for the most part, people who live abroad because they have to. Living the expatriot life in this country, in this city, means never giving up the fraternity of college life. Not fraternity like the silly Greek system, but fraternity in the real sense of the word. A brotherhood, a unity. A shared purpose, in the most existential of senses.

Here, on the cracked St. Petersburg soil, they are proud, privileged, mysterious. The slight sense of deviancy that comes from living in the land of our former enemies, the excitement of wiping their slates blank and starting fresh, the thrills from (by virtue both of necessity and adventure) committing petty crimes and minor misdemeanors on a daily basis (tax evasion, black market currency trading, small bribes, and the like)—these all contribute to a sense of cool, a sense of community, a sense of life that they cannot get back in the States, in Western Europe. Take away all that and they crumble.

In Moscow Kevin crumbled.

In Moscow he did not have his Lukes. In Moscow I was too much like home.

A few days earlier, at home in Moscow, I had sat in the kitchen. I was sitting there because Kevin was late. Like three hours late. It was night. Around ten. He wasn't answering his cell and he wasn't at work. I felt in my stomach that something was wrong.

I threw up.

Afterward, as I washed my face, as I was aggressively lathering the soap into a mask of foam, trying to cleanse myself I don't know what from, I heard his key in the door. The big, comic key. Without rinsing, I grabbed a towel, wiped myself dry, and ran to him.

"Hey!" he said and hugged me tight, so tight I could hardly breath. "I brought you a present."

And as he unloaded the flowers, the chocolates, the cookies and pastries, the *prianiki* and frozen *pel'meni* onto the kitchen table, I noticed his jeans were torn at the knee. There was blood caked around the fringing tear.

"Oh, my God. What happened?" I squatted down to inspect.

"Oh, nothing," he said, fingering the hole. "It was stupid. I tripped on the subway escalator. It's just a scrape."

"You tripped?"

"Well, I wasn't really looking."

"What were you looking at?"

He laughed and told me that he got into a fight with some kids on the platform. That they said something to him, some curse or something, and he cursed back and they starting doing that shoving thing. You know, where one guy hits the other guy's shoulder, and then the other guy hits back. But there were four of them. Four of them and one of him.

I didn't say anything. Since that e-mail I had stopped saying much.

He continued recounting the incident, not like he was scared or shaken but like he was proud. Like his adrenaline was rushing.

"And then I pushed one of them a little too hard and the fucker fell over." He was giggling, snickering, as he told me this. "And, well, it's been awhile since that black belt, you know, like ten years, so I ran. I guess there's a reason those babushkas tell you not to run on the escalator." He looked at me like he had just completed a stand-up routine, like he was waiting for my laughter or applause.

"And what's all this?" I asked, motioning toward the pile of treats on the table.

"I was missing you," he said and then grabbed me, then tossed me onto the bed.

It went on. That night went on. Nothing else really happened. and nothing else was really said. Just sex and banter and the eating of things. I haven't really even thought about it, his weird behavior, how late he was, until right now, sitting here on the bleachers, watching him and his friends as they toss the softball, cheering each other on. Outside of work, I've been trying hard not to think.

"Hey, Jen!" Kevin calls to me from left field, "come join us!" He's been trying to convince me to play all morning, but I don't really want to. I just want to sit here, quietly. So he comes to me, sits with me, arm around me, and watches for a while.

"Luke seems nice," I say.

"Luke is nice," he says.

"I like your friends."

"They like you."

And so forth. It feels good. Warm. We talk about trying to work things out so we can live in St. Petersburg someday. It is a dream we discuss from time to time. How we will live among the castles and the canals, write novels from our balcony overlooking the Neva. Not now but someday. Once we establish ourselves. Once we win the Emmys and Pulitzers. And we talk about the tsar's reburial, which will happen in a couple of months, about how we will lobby to cover it, how the network will put me up in the Hotel Astoria. The Hotel Astoria, where, as a student, I used to go to steal toilet paper from the marble bathrooms. The Hotel Astoria that looks out onto the elephantine gold dome atop St. Isaac's Cathedral.

"I want to make love to you in one of their rooms," Kevin whispers in my ear, and I laugh and say, "Me too." It always comes back to this.

It hits me now, on the bleachers, that maybe sex has become a substitute for speaking. To speak would be to acknowledge something neither of us is capable of acknowledging.

A couple of hours after the game we are sitting at a large table at the Idiot Café, eating french fries and drinking Bulgarian beer. There are a dozen of us, friends of Kevin's from the paper, from the city. Anastasia arrives, her baby in tow in a carriage. She comes to me first, kisses my cheeks.

"It's so nice to finally meet you," she says, sounding sincere. I say the same and admire the child. Try to. He does look like Kevin. Wide eyes, cowlicked hair. But then she introduces me to her husband, who is standing by her side. Maybe he looks like him. And Anastasia (I realize now that it's really true) looks a lot like me. I even say so.

"I know," she says, smiling. "I thought the same when I saw your picture." We sit down and we laugh and we compare our aquiline noses, our long brown hair, the large size of our eyes. We tease Kevin about his consistency, and he laughs and teases us back. He squeezes my hand, gives me a reassuring peck on the cheek.

We eat more fries; we drink some soda.

"A toast," says Luke, standing up.

"A toast!" they answer back.

"To Kevin, for finding such a fabulous girl!" says Luke.

Glasses clink.

"To Jennifer," says Kevin, "for being one!" They clink again; he kisses me. Anastasia kisses me. Each of his friends comes by, one by one, and kisses me.

When I look up from the adulation, I notice that all the guys have disappeared. I am sitting at a table with four women I don't really know. I know their names, sure. Anastasia, Christine, Nicole, Sara. Aside from Anastasia, they are Americans living abroad, probably because they have to. Some have known Kevin for at least a year, some longer.

They are all smiling at me, Cheshire-like.

I smile back, awkward and quizzical.

"We need to discuss something with you," they say. Anastasia says.

"Where did the guys go?" I ask. "Where's Kevin?"

"They went outside. Don't worry."

I am worried.

"Do you want something else to drink?"

"Do you want some more fries?"

Their faces telescope, like when someone gets too close to a wide-angle lens. They are distorted upon me. Suffocating.

"I want to go find Kevin," I say, but Anastasia and Nicole grab my wrists, hold me down.

"In a minute."

I look around. Out the window, in the distance, I can see him, Kevin, surrounded by the guys. Arms flailing. I see him try to push away; I see them pulling him back.

The women see me seeing him, and one of them, I don't know which one, says to me softly, "He's been drinking, Jen. He's been drinking."

I look at them, each one of them.

They tell me that he is not going to AA meetings. They tell me that friends in Moscow have seen him drunk. They tell me that he is doing drugs. Drinking and drugging.

"No," I say. "No, he isn't." I should know. I live with him. I smell him. "He's under a lot of stress, so he's just acting a little weird sometimes. You are all overreacting."

"No, Jen. No, we're not." It is Anastasia who says this. Anastasia who looks like me. Anastasia whom he loved once. Whom he still has love for. Who may or may not have snap-off panties.

"Excuse me," I say and walk outside.

You can see the dome of St. Isaac's from here, from where Kevin is sitting on the curb. And the midday sky is indeed that clichéd gray so often alluded to in the Western press. Scaffolding of never-finished construction sites holds the buildings in the background, holds the city still behind him. His face is wet. He looks at me and then closes his eyes.

"Hear them out," he says, eyes closed still.

Luke comes over and tells me how wonderful I am and how happy they are that Kevin found me. How they have all contributed money, $700, so we can go to rehab in Helsinki. He tells me that they have already called the clinic, it's a day clinic, and there is enough money for me to go with him, with Kevin, and that I must go with him, it is part of the deal, and that it is so fabulous that I can go with him and he, Luke, gives me the cash, $700 in cash, in a big round wad wrapped with a beige rubber band, and tells me to take care of it and that it would be great if we could get up to Helsinki as soon as possible. Tonight, even. And that I am wonderful. I am wonderful.

By the time he finishes, they are all here, all his friends. Circling me, praising me, thanking me. Clearly, I am absolving them of a responsibility that they have been bearing for far too long.

"Walk with me," Kevin says, sheepishly taking my hand.

"No," I say, "I need to walk alone."

This is a city of dead men, of dead men and dead souls, all alive. It is a living ghost story. There are live shadows lurking.

I am thinking, as I am walking, not of me or him or me and him but of them, the ghosts and the shadows. I think about what follows us around and from that, what we actually do see. The other day, we met a friend of Kevin's for lunch, a friend who is followed. Alexander Nikitin, a former Soviet Navy captain. He is a man with shadows. His ghosts are visible from time to time. I knew of Nikitin before I met him—before I re-met Kevin, I mean—because he, Nikitin, is famous, some might say infamous. He is a character of epic proportions, of literary worth. Enter his name in a database of newspaper articles, and you will get more hits than the system can handle.

A couple of years ago Nikitin was accused of treason. He had collaborated on an environmental report critical of the Russian Navy's nuclear waste disposal practices and was sent to prison. Because of an enormous amount of international pressure, after many, many months he was conditionally released to await a new trial. Now Nikitin lives in a Kafkaesque world filled with phone taps, surveillance, police harassment, and an endless string of court hearings. But while he shuttles from hearing to hearing and interrogation to interrogation, the number of decommissioned Russian nuclear submarines has increased dramatically, posing, according to a number of environmental groups and watchdog organizations (according to Kevin), the possibility of a Chernobyl in slow motion. If any of these submarines sink, there could be a nuclear chain reaction, and reactor accidents relating to submarines are precisely the type of problem that Nikitin was jailed and punished for talking (and continuing to talk) about.

"Kaboom!" Kevin said as he explained all this to me again. We were lying in his St. Petersburg bed the other night, sheetless because the sublessee had not yet moved all of her stuff in, but we had already moved Kevin's stuff out.

"What goes first?"

"You," he said and tickled my navel. "And then the whole St. Petersburg *oblast'*." *Oblast'* means region, as in a geographical zone.

"There go our plans for retirement."

"Eh, maybe Nikitin will save us."

"If we save him first."

Kevin had become deeply entrenched in Nikitin's case, far more than a journalist ought to, I suppose, when he first met him in jail while doing a story. Now Kevin insists that the Russian government, by trying to silence Nikitin, is trying to silence public awareness of just how dangerous their nuclear submarines and reactors might be. And, Kevin says, it is in their interest to silence any discontent—billions and billions of dollars are at stake. He tells me that the government is in the process of negotiating the sale of a number of untested reactors, and anything that taints the reputation of the reactors could be detrimental to the transactions.

I am living in newsprint.

We met Nikitin for lunch at the Idiot. He hugged us both warmly, his congratulations heartfelt. I looked at him and thought that he looked kind. I looked at how his smile lines emanated from under his thick moustache, at how his eyes were full of life even though his life was hell. His dog was beaten the other day, he told us. His dog. Can you believe it? They had taken to torturing his dog. His wife had come home to find their small white poodle limping and bloody. And he knew it was Them. He said "them" but we knew what he meant. The FSB. The old KGB. They left a message on the answering machine. Another warning. A call to be silenced, for him to stop.

He told us this in a simple way, in simple Russian, while stirring his tea. Slowly. For me, perhaps, but I think it was just his style: his exhaustion and his exasperation.

Kevin placed a hand on top of his, calmed the stirring, and Nikitin relaxed for a moment.

We left the cafe and walked him to his car.

The tires were slashed. All four of them.

A noise, a clap, called us to attention, to turn. Down the street stood two uniformed men. Men in dark uniforms, standing, legs spread for a moment, for us to see, to watch as they got into a car and sped off.

"You see," Nikitin said to me softly, resigned.

Slowly, we moved away from his shadows.

And now I am thinking as I am walking, is this why I am here? Am I supposed to help Kevin so he can help Nikitin save the world? Is that what's going on? I think about the missionary on the plane, the one with the spearmint gum and the blue cardigan. I think about God's will, and I thing about willingness and willfulness and the willies.

Then I think, that's absurd. I am absurd. This whole thing is absurd. I laugh and I kick a stone and then another one down the embankment into the murky waters of the Neva River, along which I am walking now.

My mind is tripping, racing. I am thinking of things. I am thinking of everything and of nothing. Sounds, songs, meanings. I think of jumping in and jumping off, and I think of going home and I think of staying. I am running now. Trotting, really. Trying to focus, trying to unscatter scattered thoughts. Trotting along the path between the river and the road, crossing the cracked sidewalks that lead over bridges, across canals. The canals that drowned the bones and the broken spirits. I think of Russia and of Russian. I think of words.

Embankment, I think.

I think of how, when you learn a new language with a mind already formed, words often conjure memories before they conjure meanings. For me, the Russian word for *embankment* is one of those. *Naberezhnaia.* And as I trot, now walk, along the embankment, moving with no specific destination but simply the desire to get away, to not be near his friends, his cafe, his city, I cannot think about the horribleness of what has just occurred. To digest the intervention would be to attempt to comprehend it. Instead, my mind is rushing into a regressive state, reciting odd tongue twisters and pulling pictures of the most irrelevant things into focus. A window I once saw in France. A cat that was hanging off a balcony in Puerto Rico. Vocabulary words on index cards. *Embankment. Naberezhnaia.*

It was a word I learned the summer after my junior year of college. The summer before I met Kevin, when I was living with Vera, who was sleeping with Boris, who was married to Tanya, who was living with Efonya, and so forth. Where was I? I was studying at the Pushkin Institute in what was then called Leningrad. The institute was on a side street behind the Kazan Cathedral, a gargantuan gray structure that is surrounded by a fortress of ninety-six columns. It was built at the beginning of the nineteenth century to house the icon of the miracle-working Lady of Kazan. By the year I was studying at the institute, the Kazankski Sobor was better known for housing the Museum to Atheism.

The cool platforms between the corroding columns were and are a central congregating point for the city's youth. The columns provide shadows to neck in and wind shelters for cigarettes and drugs. You have to be careful not to trip over strewn-about beer bottles and broken glass when passing by. I learned this one rainy day when flipping index cards as I crammed for the weekly vocabulary test.

"Embankment," I read on the unlined side and then briefly closed my eyes as I tried to relieve my constipated brain.

Suddenly, my blind foot rolled across a loose bottle and slipped out from under me. I landed, legs splayed out like a little girl playing jacks, index cards scattered about in front of me. I absorbed the shock, gathered myself to a squatting position, and contemplated gathering the words. One white 3 x 5 was flirtatiously teasing the edge of a puddle to my right, so I leaned over to grab it first. *Naberezhnaia*, I read again when I picked it up. I turned the card over. *Embankment*.

And here, almost seven years later, I am walking along a quiet length of the Moika Naberezhnaia, not a ten-minute walk from the cathedral (now home to religious services and a museum of Soviet memorabilia). A word. *Bereg*, I think. The bank, like of a river, an embankment. *Na beregu reki.*

There is a popular Russian folk song about a young girl strolling along a riverbank, singing because she has received a letter from her fiancé, a soldier off at war, off to protect their country, their world, their dreams. She sings to him, hoping her words of love will fly on the backs of the birds. It's a nice song, and chances are you will hear it anytime you are sitting around a campfire with a bunch of Russian friends or are getting drunk with some provincial strangers as you travel on the overnight train from Moscow to St. Pete. They usually teach the song in first-year Russian classes and rightly so. It is catchy and easy, and it makes you feel good.

I hum the tune as I kick at the pebbles strewn about the dirty path, just up from the edge of the canal.

> *Rastsvetali iabloni i grushi,*
> *Poplili tumani nad rekoi.*
> *Vykhodila na bereg Katiusha,*
> *Na vysokii bereg, na krutoi.*
>
> [The apples and pears were growing,
> The fog was spreading over the river.
> Katusha walked along the bank,
> On the high bank, on the edge.]

I decide to go with Kevin to Helsinki because I can't think of a good reason not to. Because, truth be told, I can't really think.

20

St. petersburg—A couple of hours later I am back at the apartment, inside the former castle of the serfs. I find Kevin sitting on the balcony overlooking the feral garden, smoking his L&Ms. Luke is dragging heavy trunks across the living room, scraping up the centuries-old wood, helping to rearrange things for Lucy, the plump British woman who is taking over the lease. I go to Luke, or maybe he comes to me. He gives me a hug and I tell him I am OK. That everything will be OK. Kevin remains on the outside, not acknowledging my return, but then again, I am not acknowledging him. And Lucy, who knows nothing, is unpacking her sheets, placing them neatly folded into the cabinet.

The phone rings, the bulbous yellow rotary phone with its awful grating screech that demands the immediate attention of everyone in the room. Kind of like a fire alarm.

"I'll get it!" Kevin shouts and rushes to pick it up. He gets it before the second ring.

"Alo?" he says.

Luke whispers to me that Kevin has been waiting for the bureau chief of the Associated Press to call him back, for a job. Another job.

Because the *Newsday* thing is just for the summer, he told Luke. Because he doesn't think it is prestigious enough.

"Prestigious enough for whom?" I ask, meaning it to be rhetorical.

"He said for you."

I smile weakly to show Luke that I understand what he means, even though I don't. Not really. I look at Kevin's hand clenched tightly around the receiver, white knuckled. Maybe I did do something wrong. Maybe he mistook ambition and admiration for pressure and presumption.

Kevin's voice is cracking, weak. Clearly, things aren't going well. Suddenly, the receiver hits the table. The phone itself smashes into the dingy, faded yellow-papered wall, then bounces across the floor, ringing for help throughout the duration of its flight. The whole apartment is animated, like a force has taken over. Objects crash in the kitchen. The front door slams open and jumps off its hinges.

An abrupt silence falls over the room.

Kevin is gone.

Lucy, Luke, and I look at each other, stunned. They wait for my reaction, but I have none.

Then I smile meekly. I sigh.

"Luke," I say, "would you mind trying to find Kevin? I am afraid he might do something stupid, and we have a bus to catch in a few hours."

I turn to Lucy. "I am really sorry you have to deal with this."

She gives me a stiff hug around my shoulders, like she thinks it is the proper thing to do.

I manage to reassemble the fractured phone and call the bureau. I tell Sylvia that my fiancé needs emergency surgery in Helsinki. She doesn't ask any questions but says that they will help me negotiate the reentry visa. I call my parents to tell them . . . something. I don't know what.

"Hi," I say into their answering machine. "I just wanted to let you know I am, I mean, we are going to Helsinki. I have to renew my visa. We'll be back in Moscow in about a week. Love you." I hang up, but it feels all wrong. I pick up the chunky yellow receiver again and redial. This time my mother answers.

"Hello? Hello?"

"Hi, Mom. It's me. Can you hear me?"

"Jen! Hold on a second. We just walked in. Let me change phones. Here. Is that better? Jen?"

"Yes. I'm here." I have to hold the cord in its socket at the base of the phone or the connection fizzes out. So I am sitting here, holding it just so, wanting but not able to reach down to slap Kesha, who is rubbing up against my legs, leaving tracks of fur across my pants. I kick him instead.

"You sound so far away."

"I am so far away, Mom."

"I mean, farther than usual. Where are you calling from?"

"We are in St. Pete."

"Why does it sound so funny?"

"Mom, I—"

"Oh, listen. I am so glad you called. We need to make a decision about the tablecloths for the wedding."

"Mom—" I can feel a lump emerge, like a cancerous growth in the back of my throat.

"Rachel and I narrowed it down to two swatches, but I was hoping I could FedEx them to you so you can have the final say. Although your father thinks you'd prefer the forest green over the burgundy."

"Mom, I can't—" I close my eyes and try to swallow. I breathe in deeply, and I can smell the dust in the corners of the apartment, the overflowing ashtray at the edge of the table. I can feel my tears clinging to the tiny hairs on my cheeks, and then I taste them as they tumble into the crevices of my mouth.

"OK. We'll just flip a coin. But personally I think the—"

"No. I mean, I can't. I'm so sorry. I—"

"You what? Are you crying? Jenabeth, what's wrong? Oh, my God. Richard! Pick up the phone!"

"Hello?" my father says.

"Jennifer's on the line. Something's wrong."

"Mom, it's—shit." Loud static comes across the line as I wipe my nose against the back of my hand.

"What?" I hear them say as I fiddle the cord back into place. "What's wrong?"

I exhale, audibly. "We need to postpone the wedding."

"What?"

"We need to postpone the wedding." I realize this is the first time I have actually thought this at all, but saying it, it makes sense. It feels awful, but it also feels right.

"I can't hear you. Pull yourself together. Take a deep breath. There. Now, what did you say?"

"Daddy, we need to postpone the wedding."

"Oh, shit. Richard, let me talk to her."

"No! Dad, stay on the phone. Please." I am sobbing.

"What happened?" says my father. "Are you OK? Stop it. Pull yourself together. OK? What happened?"

"I lied to you, Daddy. We aren't just going to Helsinki to renew my visa. Well, we are, but there is another reason. Kevin needs to go into rehab."

"Oh, my god! Is he drinking? Is he doing drugs?" My mother.

"Has he hurt you?" My father.

"Oh, my God. OK. Wait. Jen, take a deep breath. Please. Stop crying. It's OK. We'll get the deposit back. Don't worry. It will be OK." Both of them.

"I'm scared." I blurt this out like a little girl might, one who, having falling off the swing set, has unsuccessfully held back her tears.

"Do you want me to come get you?" my mother says. "What's the number for Delta? I'll get on the next flight."

"No, it's OK." And anyway, I think, you can't just come to Russia like that. You need to apply for a visa, to wait for a few days. I roll my watery eyes at no one, and it calms me down a bit. "I just needed you to know." I don't know why I told them right now, in the middle of all this. I can feel the panic in their voices, their overwhelming concern. I guess I called them because I didn't know whom else to call. Maybe calling them makes it real. "It's all fine, really. It's OK," I say to them, to myself, and I try to muffle my sniffling by holding the receiver away from my mouth.

My parents say they want me to come home immediately, but I can't. Back there all I have are friends who will say I told you so, and a demoralizing crawl back to my old boss, tail between my legs. Here, I still have the hope of us, even if we are tainted.

"The wedding's not off," I tell them once my eyes have drained. "It's just being postponed. If anyone asks, just tell them the political situation in Russia is too heated and we need to be here. For our careers."

I have become someone who lives abroad not because she wants to but because she has to.

Luke returns alone, concerned. He sits down with me in the living room, at the same table where a few months back Kevin and I interviewed the prostitute. But this time we are quiet, so lost for words that it feels almost like we are sitting shiva, that we are in mourning, except that Lucy is methodically dusting and unpacking her bags around us.

Then we hear him. We hear him walk into the kitchen and fill up the rusty bathtub that stands by the stove. We are paralyzed, afraid to approach. We hear him close the door to the kitchen and step into the tub. By the time I open the door, there is complete silence except for the running water.

The first thing I notice is his knees. He is lying half-submerged in the tub which cannot hold him. I watch as the water drops from the faucet and forces a turbulence around him. The water swirls wildly around his limbs, and a few beads grab onto the sparse hairs of his chest. I fear following the lines of the veins in his neck. They would lead me to his eyes, and his eyes would tell me everything I don't want to know.

I stand still and do not speak. I absorb the rhythm of the blood (my fiancé's blood) as it pulsates into the water. The blood swims in a steady dark stream from his wrist, down the palm of his hand. Slowly, it pools at his fingertips and then dives into the spiraling swirl.

"I am filling the tub so I don't make a mess," he whispers as if to no one.

I don't say anything. I know what he is doing.

"Let me give you some advice, Jen," he says. "Go home." He pauses a moment and says, "You can't last in Russia. You don't belong here. Go home." Then he takes the knife and tries to carve some more.

Shock is a funny thing. It's like a circuit shorting out. I want to say so many things.

Don't do it.

Stop it.

Fine, kill yourself.

Asshole, that knife is as sharp as a stick of butter. Let me find you a razor.

I don't know how to call for an ambulance.

I can't live without you.

Fuck you.

You've ruined my life.

I curse the day I met you.

You selfish prick.

You pig-headed bastard.

I love you.

I don't say anything at all.

Instead, I stand static for what feels like a year but is probably about three seconds. A molasses moment. I stare at the man I have promised my life to. He looks scared and skinny and absolutely strange. I watch his blood continue to form intricate patterns as it trickles into the rusty water. It reminds me of that beautiful Italian paper they sell by the Ponte Vecchio Bridge in Florence. And, as has become my habit of late, I bite the diamond ring.

I walk out of the room and tell Luke to please take care of his friend. Right now, I cannot.

21

We wanted piercing anguish
Instead of placid happiness . . .
I won't abandon my comrade,
So dissolute and mild.
       Anna Akhmatova, 1889–1966

O N T H E B O R D E R —The bus to Helsinki leaves just after
11 P.M. It quietly sidles up the corner of the Bolshaya
Morskaya embankment at about a quarter to. The bus
driver sits stoically behind his wheel, doors locked, while passengers
gather on the windy unlit street. "This feels like a stealth runaway op-
eration," I whisper to Kevin as our taxi drives up behind the swollen,
dirt-encased bumper. We get out of the car, and I lift the bags from
the trunk, my acceptance of the lack of chivalry an homage to the
wounded wrists, wrists sliced but not severed, veins still pumping
through to palms. Luke had tied him up in rags and stopped the
bleeding. The only thing that was really lost down the drain was some
pride. Mine, not Kevin's. Kevin seems oblivious to the gravity of
events. But he is impatient and distracted and insists on running to
get some cigarettes at the round-the-clock store across the way. The

narrow bus door swings open in front of me. I climb in, claim two seats, roll my bulky sweater into a lumpy pillow, and close my eyes.

I open them when the smell of stale smoke from Kevin's jacket penetrates my space. He plops himself down.

"Hey, there," he says in that voice that once turned me on. Hey, there, like a raspy movie star, like an artist worn from work. Hey, there, like a secret code, a pact, or a poem.

I don't respond.

With a callused finger he combs a strand of hair away from my face. His fingernails are clean from the hours of soaking. I can smell the soap saturated beneath the skin, almost—but not quite—masking the indelible nicotine perfume on his hands. I don't want to see them, his hands. I don't want to see the stained gauze on his wrists, so I shut my eyes again, hoping to pass for sleeping.

He snuggles up and puts his head on my shoulder.

I push him away. "You are acting like a puppy who just peed on the rug," I say.

He whimpers.

"That's not cute." I turn to the window.

He whimpers again, and I surrender as he returns his head to my shoulder.

The bus starts and we lurch forward, fall back into place.

We wind our way past the canals and archways of the city, the shadows so extreme that they recall the *Cabinet of Dr. Caligari* or some other early black-and-white horror movie. Sharp dark angles. Ominous streaks of black. I shiver.

"What's wrong?" he says, trying again to brush back my hair. I swat at his hand and then immediately worry that I may have hurt him.

"Oh, my god, I'm sorry," I say, resting my hand on his, which has fallen to my knee.

"What?"

"Did I hit the cut?"

He looks at me like I am nuts, like there are no cuts, no bloodied bandages, no stained egos.

The disconnect between us is so great that when he leans over to kiss me, I am not even surprised. We're just operating on totally different planes. I feel the bandage brush up against my waist as his fingers fumble for my zipper, and I surrender again.

My friend Olga once said that erotica is just a depository of pain. Or something like that. If you are fully contented in a relationship, in life, there is no need to act out sexually deviant fantasies, she said. When life is good, sex should be sweet and kind.

"Perhaps," I told her. Perhaps, I am thinking now.

Kevin's calloused fingers snake through the coarse tangle of my pubic hair until, finally, one finds its way to the proper place. It lingers there for a moment. A soft stroke, circling.

It surprises me how wet I am, how turned on. I hate him right now. I hate him for toying so closely with death and then, not more than a few hours later, doing this—toying with me. But as his fingers slip deeper inside me, I let go.

We don't speak.

I can't look at him.

I stare through the fogging window at the cracks in the buildings and the streetlamp-lit potholes. Occasionally, we go over one, forcing him deeper into me for a moment, causing me to cum faster than I would like.

This goes on until we reach the border.

He takes his hand out from inside me and when he holds his passport out to the customs agent, I can see a wet spot on the front. When the agent returns the passport, Kevin looks into my eyes and licks the cover dry.

"Charming," I say and get up to follow the other travelers off the bus for the rest of the inspection at the border check.

The Finnish guards need to run everyone's luggage through the x-ray machine, our bodies through a metal detector, but leaving Russia takes no time at all.

On the other side, past the uniformed men whose job it is to see us through, there are shelves filled with glossy circulars, like the kind you might find at the exit of a Price Chopper supermarket. Coupons for hotels, lawn furniture, cars. Anything and everything. There is a functional soda machine filled with Coke, Diet Coke. They even have 7-Up.

"I think we just walked into Kmart," says Kevin.

He is disparaging.

I am thrilled.

"Let's buy some plastic lawn furniture as soon as we get to Helsinki," I say, smiling, happy under the bright fluorescent bulbs, more comfortable than I have felt in months. I pass him a well-printed brochure advertising plastic deck chairs with matching patio umbrellas.

He takes my hand instead and smiles. "We are going to be OK, right?" He kisses my cheek and thanks me.

"For what?" I ask.

"For you."

I am crying, I think. It feels like I'm crying, although when I feel for them, there are no tears.

The bus pulls into the Helsinki station at the break of dawn. The streets are quiet, but occasionally a car splashes through one of the scattered puddles that litter the ground. Kevin moves assuredly; he knows his way around. He has been to this rehab before, he tells me now. We walk through the empty city to our hotel, the sun rising with each step, our feet slapping wet cement.

We breathe.

Helsinki air is so crisp and clean that I have to draw hard to get a lung full, to make it stick. It is so clear that I can make out details on buildings as far as I can see, regardless of the dirt on my contact lenses.

Kevin lights a cigarette.

"Can you blow that in another direction?" I say.

"I can't direct the wind," he says, surly.

Some thanks. I move upwind of him. "We aren't OK," I say.

"What?" he says, not hearing.

We have been here three days now, and we have moved from the nice, well-appointed Marriott clone by the marina to the shabby, moldy youth hostel up the hill. The $700 has turned to $300 with very few words spoken.

This is a day:

We wake up and I walk with him to his meeting. On the way we stop off at a pharmacy because he needs a refill on his Valium. I refrain from making an observation, a comment, an accusation. I drop him off on the corner. I sit in cafes. I look at the street signs with their incomprehensibly long Finnish words. I go to the movies. I buy clothing on credit and write postcards home, telling everyone how lovely it is to be in a Western town, how good it is to have a proper cup of coffee. The sun doesn't set until nearly midnight, and it rises just hours later, so when Kevin meets me in the evening and we stroll in the gardens and along the waterfront, when we sit in the parks, we can see everything.

The clarity confuses me.

"Are you—?" I begin to ask.

He rolls over in the grass, toward me. His hair is overgrown, sticking out from under his dark, dirty knit cap like stubborn weeds. His facial hair is transitioning to a blotchy, uneven beard.

"Am I what?" he says.

"Is there something you need me to know?"

"Like what?"

I don't know like what. Should he tell me about his day, about rehab? Should he tell me why the Valium keeps running out, why his face is swollen? why his skin is yellowish? Should I ask?

It occurs to me, staring up into the clear Helsinki sky as we are lying on the manicured lawn behind our cheap hostel, holding hands but not feeling them, that I am indeed living my life according to his family's script. I imagine the tight shot on the screen, the stage directions written in the center of the page. Fights are solved with kisses, and feelings dissolve from bad to good and back at thirty frames a second. Occasionally, there are hard edits. I am living my life as an out-of-body experience. It is a classic movie, a literary fable. Just the other week, a guy I work with at the bureau told me that I am like a character out of a nineteenth-century novel. "Who isn't?" I said, sort of flattered, sort of offended. And now I think, lying here, isn't this what I wanted?

"Are you feeling any better?" I finally ask. "Is outpatient rehab working at all?"

He laughs and says, "To tell you the truth, I think it is a crock of shit."

I am silent, so he strokes my forehead and says it's OK, though. He doesn't really need it; he just needed to get away.

"But where did you need to go?"

There is silence, strained. There is an unmade bed with twisted, sweat-drenched sheets. There are no plans, no propositions. He goes to the meetings; I go to the consulate. My papers are delayed, they tell me, and I will have to stay in town one day longer. I will have to stay alone in Helsinki, and he will go back, to work, to live, to continue.

Tomorrow.

I walk back to the hostel, and blood is no longer pumping inside me. Through my emptying vessels I feel instead a black thick sludge, an oozing force that slowly, methodically, works its way around my gut, through my nerves and cells. I cannot cry. I cannot eat. But I know this feeling. This is the feeling that used to force me to purge. To binge so that I could vomit it all up. This is the feeling that I used to get when I was younger, before the Prozac. Before the therapy. Before. A feeling akin to panic but more methodical, if that makes any sense at all. A feeling of an interior vortex sucking me into myself. It is an emptiness one step beyond. This, I imagine, is the feeling that he has too. Now. This is the feeling that makes him drink or drug or do whatever it is that he is doing. And I know he is doing. I know it. And if he can do it, I can do it too.

I toss back my tangled hair, wrist rubbing snot from my dripping nose. In our room I open his brown leather toiletry bag, that Pandora's box. Do you want to refill the Valium again? And again? Two can play this game, love. We really can. We can do this all together now, because I just don't want to be alone.

22

Moscow—It is May. It is June. It is July. The Russian stock market is teetering on the brink of collapse, the MIR space station is experiencing computer failures, Yeltsin is courting Serbian war criminals, bombs are exploding in Moscow synagogues, and Vice President Al Gore is coming to visit. American editorials argue about who is losing Russia and Russian editorials argue the same. Read the papers, and the world is at end.

Ask your Russian friends, and they laugh and ask you to please pass the sugar. Ask the guy sitting next to you on the metro and he stares at you, blankly.

Ask me or Kevin, and we are just doing our jobs. We are just trying to hold it together, put on a good face.

This is a day:

I hit the snooze bar a dozen times, and when I finally roll out of bed, I don't know which to grab first, the codeine or the coffee. My head hurts. My eyes are heavy. Sometimes he boils the water, sometimes I do.

There is no hot water now, in July. The pipes are old—many date to Stalin's era. The pipes, says the Water Ministry, need rest, so we are forced to bucket-brigade small saucepans of stove-boiled water from kitchen to bathroom and back again. We step through a gauntlet of wallpaper rolls and pieces of plywood, trying not to spill. Some days we wash together. Some days we don't wash at all. And it is those days, the grungy days, when things feel more proper. Washing, preening, scrubbing backs—those are actions of lovers, actions too affirmative when there is too little to affirm.

I take my coffee in a travel mug and I leave.

On the metro I don't talk to the guy next to me. I don't ask him any questions. Instead, in these jostled sardine-packed minutes, I ruminate. I think about politics and polemics and professional aspirations. I think about drugs and disgrace and deception.

I was deceived, I think. Not by Kevin. It is not his fault, exactly. He was deceived too. We were deceived by our fantasies, our hyperactive imaginations, and an unfounded optimism fueled by a lifetime of fairy tales, Hollywood movies, and classic novels that romanticize tragedy and deify the power of romance. And when I look at the teenage girl sitting opposite me, the one with the perfectly coiffed hair and delicately lined eyes, I want to grab the tabloid that she is reading, the one with celebrities on the cover, the one with the double-page horoscope spread and the Dear Abby type of advice. I want to take her and shake her and turn her to face the old lady sitting next to her, the one with the torn stockings and the breasts to her knees. But then I think, no. Let her live in that world for a while. Let her enjoy it while it lasts. I know that I don't know the answer. I don't know what I would tell this girl, if I were actually given the opportunity. I don't know what to tell myself.

There was a poll done recently. It stated that prostitution ranks among the top ten career aspirations of Russian girls, and I am unclear whether this is their fantasy or reality.

In my reality I am soon sitting in a marble bathroom stall at the Slavyanskaya Hotel. My cell phone rings as I reach for the toilet paper. It is a pimp named Pasha, and the irony is not lost on me at all that, as I chat with him from the stall, real prostitutes are chatting

174

with their *sutenër,* their pimps, in the stalls next to me, up by the mirror, and in the lobby of the hotel.

"Can I call you back?" I say in Russian. "This is not a very good place for me to talk." I haven't even wiped yet.

"Net," he says. He won't give me a number. So we agree to meet in the evening at a cafe near Tsvetnoy Boulevard, just up from the Circus, and I wonder why everything in my life has to be such a damn metaphor.

Pasha traffics in young girls. I was introduced to him by Yulia, who knew him through a friend from the modeling agency she works for. The same friend who hooked her up with freelance work translating porn videos from English to Russian. Kevin and I assisted her on the first project a little over a month ago, when we first returned from Helsinki.

That day we sat in a small office near the Kutuzovsky Bridge, curtains closed so that there was no glare on the screen. Kevin had been reluctant to join us at first, but even though my Russian was getting stronger, I was pretty sure I wouldn't know the correct words for the slang. I convinced him to come by way of whining and guilt. Guilt has become my currency.

"I was thinking of going for a walk after work," he said.

"And me?" I answered.

So he came along to translate bad movies in a darkened room. In there, in the dark, we held hands and laughed and contemplated the proper translations of cock-sucking expletives and donkey-hung grunts. It wasn't the perversion; it was the consolation. In front of these actors, confronted by their horrendous poses and prose, we felt stronger, more substantive. Deep. Our love wasn't about whips and chains. Our erotica needed no props. When Yulia pushed the eject button with her sinewy finger, we asked her to please invite us again.

There was something in the aftermath of that afternoon that hung over us for a few days. We went out for walks and for talks, and for a little while we were OK.

For a few days we were a couple. We scrubbed each other's back and we fell asleep unassisted.

"I have a surprise for you," Kevin would say to me over the phone. "Come meet me after work." And I did. He took my hand and I walked with him.

"We are going to celebrate," he said, weaving us around a sea of Mercedeses and Range Rovers parked on the street.

"Celebrate what?" I said.

"That we are going to be OK."

We went to Shinok, one of many new theme restaurants that had cropped up to feed and entertain Moscow's New Rich. It looked like a Ukrainian hunting lodge on steroids. We entered through a giant wooden Flintstonesque door and proceeded up two flights of bloated stairs to the dining room, which surrounded an actual working farm, encased in glass: a horse, goats, chickens, even a small wrinkled babushka who picks up after the animals. And it was nice. We ate heavy food and asked the waiter in the embroidered peasant shirt about employment at the farm.

We laughed.

We held hands when we walked home.

But that was weeks ago. We have since slipped back into our post-Helsinki stupor. We pop pills, too paralyzed to do much more, believing that, somehow, by numbing time, time will pass and things will heal. But I know this is not enough, I know I want more. I want back what we never really had. I want our fantasies.

So now I am sitting in the bathroom stall at the Radisson Slavyanskaya. I call him and ask him to join me with Pasha.

"Can't you do your own stories?" he says.

"Jesus. I thought it might be fun."

"I don't feel like fun. I feel like going home after work." This is what we do. We go home after work. We silently skulk about the apartment. He goes on cigarette runs, and I compose cunningly upbeat e-mails to send back home. We take sleeping pills and codeine and call it a day.

I say, "Fine," and go it alone to hang out with a man who traffics in young girls. I have no idea why Pasha is even willing to work with me, except that it might be a favor to Yulia, but I have no idea what the hell he might owe her for, except that, as she herself surmised, he might see her as a potential conduit to young models who also dream of being whores, just like the rest of the high school girls who have their fantasies all confused. And I am beginning to think that Yulia, by involving herself with pimps and prostitutes and porn, is trading in some sort of detached illusion. That to make her life interesting, palatable (a life that involves sharing a two-room apartment with her parents, her brother, rotating refugee relatives from Baku, and two cats), she too must write herself a dramatic script.

Pasha arrives at the cafe just a few minutes late. He is short and bearded and looks more rabbinical than unethical. Yulia is with him, tall and angular and dressed in black. The three of us sit on stools and make small talk as we sip the watery espressos that I paid for. It turns out that Yulia and Pasha went to the same high school, a couple of years apart—Pasha is younger—and for a few moments they reminisce about this teacher, that classroom.

We banter and gossip and even crack jokes.

"Two girls are talking," says Pasha. "'I'm going to marry a man I fall in love with,' says the first one. 'Me too,' says the other, 'if I don't find anything better.'"

"Which brings us to the subject at hand," I say, compelling Pasha to pull out a Kodak envelope. He displays the stack of photographs like a proud parent.

"Isn't she beautiful?" he says, passing me a 4 x 5 glossy print of a blond girl in a blue bikini. She is sitting on a white enamel table, the kind you might find in a kitchen. "This is Zhana," he says. "And this is Ilana." He passes me another one. And then another. "They are all straight-A students, very bright. Sveta here is a talented painter."

"Why are they doing this, then?" I say.

He laughs, like it's so obvious, like he shouldn't have to answer. So I look to Yulia.

"The good life," she says, shrugging her shoulders.

"They don't want to be streetwalkers," says Pasha, "they are looking for something more high class." Short of a sugar daddy, he explains, they don't have other options. And he has a point. Yulia works a more or less honest job and hasn't been paid in months, except when translating porn. Elena's husband, Mikhail, took home a frozen salmon last week instead of a salary. Russian kids watch their parents slave for nothing, and then they turn on the television and see repeats of *Dynasty*. Walking in the streets of central Moscow, they see mink-clad women insert stiletto-heeled feet into limousines. When the cars pull away, they see beggars.

"And they'll talk to me? on camera?" I ask, handing back the stack. I am having trouble looking at the pictures.

"They will if I ask them to," he says.

We finish our drinks and leave the cafe, the three of us, and walk in the direction of Red Square. It is dark and cool and quiet on the street, but the path to the city center is well marked by the neon signs beckoning us into strip joints and casinos. As we get closer, we hear a growing roar, like that of a crowd, an audience. A loud crack—it sounds like a gunshot—stops us cold, but we quickly realize that it is not a shower of bullets that we are about to witness but fireworks. Red and white fireflies splashing down over the cupolas. Blue glitter coating the Kremlin gates. A drum roll, an electronic pulse, and we are standing at the top of Tverskaya, the main avenue leading to the square, the avenue lined with furs and diamonds, with Lancôme and Versace and Hugo Boss. From here we can see a sea of people gyrating in front of Lenin's Tomb, we can hear the synthetic beat of Europop.

"What the hell?" I say in English.

"Bozhe moi," says Yulia. My God.

Pasha apprehends a boy who is trotting past, a teenager with spiked hair and baggy jeans, and asks him if he knows what's going on. It's Independence Day, the boy tells us, and *Molotok Magazine* is sponsoring a party on the square.

We laugh at our ignorance. It's like forgetting the Fourth of July. Yulia sighs and says that when she was younger, she always knew every holiday, every celebration. Pasha says that he used to march on

Red Square as a kid. He knew how to tie his Pioneer scarf and how to keep lockstep with the rest of the marching Komosomolets, but he never understood what he was celebrating.

"Wait a second," he says. "Independence Day was last month, I think. It's in June." Yulia laughs and say, yeah, that seems correct.

"Do you think any of these kids know what they are celebrating?" I ask.

"Yes," he says, "they are celebrating the free Pepsis they are handing out."

When we reach the square five minutes later, the party is already over, and armed police officers are herding the crowds out into the street, down into the metro. There are thousands of boys and girls, mostly teenagers, high off the beat, the pulse, the spectacular displays of light. Some have neon necklaces and others wave flags. They are laughing and shouting and just carrying on, just being teenagers.

"Any one of these girls would consider working with me," Pasha says as we press ourselves up against the cold stones of a building to avoid being overrun.

"What do you offer them?"

"A rich boyfriend. A sponsor, a *papik*." A sugar daddy. "Watch," he says, tugging down the elasticized waist of his brown leather bomber jacket. He steps forward and gingerly plucks two girls from the crowd. They seem startled at first, but they hear him out. He speaks softly, conspiratorially, a few too many feet away for us to hear. Yulia and I watch as the girls' body language changes—from crossed arms and a distant stance to hands in back pockets, torsos leaning in. They look, well, like teenage girls, teenage girls anywhere in the world, with tight T-shirts, ponytails, and jeans. There is nothing special about them, nothing to suggest that they aspire to be whores or, the reverse, that they don't.

Pasha returns to us, triumphant. They took his card; they expressed interest. He is confident they will call.

"How old are they?" I ask.

"They say sixteen," he says. "But I think fourteen is more accurate."

Pasha promises to ring later in the week to set a time for me to interview some of his girls, perhaps even go to school with them, go home to meet their families.

"Their parents are OK with this?" I say.

"Ask them," he says, and we step into the stream of people undulating toward the Revolution Square metro stop.

On the train I am again stuck in my head, stuck staring at the kids sitting opposite me, stuck thinking about how bizarre it is that a pimp just kissed my cheek, how at the age of fourteen my dreams of the future had more to do with foreign travel, fabulous adventures, fun and games. I don't think I even knew what a sugar daddy was at that age, much less a high-class whore.

I miss my stop at Pushkinskaya and have to keep going to Belorusskaya to switch to the line that will take me home. Skipping stops. Fast forwarding and needing to carefully rewind. It really does all rest on clichés. Platitudes are profound. Early birds and tortoises win. Jump-start a relationship, jump-start adulthood, jump-start a democracy—the results are the same. Kevin and I are no different than these girls, than this country. We are no different than the network news with its slap-shot coverage, the obviousness of its questions, its inabilities to explore real answers. Our union is the same as the beasts that brought us together. It was spun from the same cheap disintegrating fabric, once shiny with its intoxicating design.

And so now, headed back in the proper direction, I start to think about fairy tales and fables and false promises. I think about a fairy tale that I recently read to Elena's son.

Once upon a time there lived a fool named Emelya who slept on the stove all day long. One day, when Emelya went to the ice hole for water, he caught a golden pike. The fish said if he let her go, she would grant any of his wishes. "Just say these magic words: 'By the pike's wish, at my command,' and everything will be done," the pike said. So Emelya let the fish go and then ordered his water pails to go home by themselves, which they did. Then he ordered the sledge to go by itself to the nearest forest, and his ax chopped wood for the fire.

The tsar of the land heard about this wonder and sent his officer to bring Emelya to the palace. When Emelya came to the tsar's courtyard, he saw the tsar's daughter and used the pike's magic to make her fall in love with him.

The tsar was angry that his daughter did not fall in love with a prince, so he gave orders to place the princess and Emelya in a barrel and throw them into the sea. Emelya again used the magic words, and the waves rolled the barrel onto the shore of a beautiful island. With the pike's help Emelya built a big marble palace.

Then the princess asked him to become handsome and smart, and he turned himself into a fine young prince. They started to live peacefully in the palace.

One day the tsar visited the island and recognized his own daughter and Emelya. The tsar wept and asked their forgiveness. They celebrated the family's reunion and lived happily ever after.

Riding up the endless escalator at the Krasnopresnyenskaya metro stop—the correct stop—I wonder what I would ask the golden fish. If I asked for love and success, for success in love and success in my career, how could I ever trust that I actually deserved them? And, not deserving, how could I possibly appreciate anything? And without appreciating anything, everything will fall apart.

I don't know what to ask for.

Later, at home, I ask Kevin to pass the salt. I am sitting at our kitchen table, trying to eat some eggs. He is smoking a cigarette and staring out the window, the one with the prisonlike iron bars that faces the front of the prosecutor's office. He doesn't respond, and I am not sure whether he didn't hear me or if he is just being an ass. I ask again, because the shaker is on the counter next to where he stands, and he then hands it to me, slow motion, and says "sorry" so softly that I am uncertain whether he said it at all.

"Do you want some?" I say, gingerly pushing the plate toward him.

"No, thanks. I'm not hungry," he says.

Neither am I, not for food. I am hungry for an answer, for a deeper response or resolution. For an end or a beginning. For time to no longer be a dull blur of pain, broken up by days at work, stuttered by the elusive fantasies of prostitutes, politics, and promotions.

I can't recall the last real conversation we had, and I am starting to wonder whether we ever even had one at all.

"How was work?" I say.

"Fine," he answers.

"Did you go?"

"No."

"Did you get to your A.A. meeting?"

"No."

I watch him, now standing next to me, now hovering over the table. Like maybe he wants the eggs, but he isn't sure, and the decision is too complicated to complete. He is frozen. A bloated, unwashed man, frozen inside a space he does not own. Gently, I place my hand on his wrist, now scarred over.

He snaps it away. As if I were a bug crawling, something poisonous, about to bite.

"What?"

"Leave me alone!" he says, shouting it as if I were attacking him, raping him, doing something unthinkable. But as he says this, shouts this, he looks as stunned as I feel. Stunned by the suddenness of the outburst and by the content and anger of his words.

My pager starts to vibrate against my waist, tickling me a little. A text message asks me to return to the bureau. New York wants a package for the morning show because the billionaire financier George Soros is calling for a devaluation of the ruble.

I don't understand much about economics, but I do understand that this isn't good. I understand a ruble devaluation would be disastrous for the many Russian corporations that have borrowed in dollars and that it would probably result in the collapse of the Russian banking system. But I also know that the Russian banking system is, to all intents and purposes, pretty well wiped out. So, really, what Soros is asking for is to call a spade a spade. The ruble is worthless, he's saying. Let's just face facts.

I look at Kevin, my fiancé. A fiancé without a wedding date, a lover without love.

He is staring blankly at the salt that took such strength to move.

"I am going back to the office," I say.

23

Moscow — This is a week: President Clinton is preparing to testify in front of a grand jury, terrorists are bombing American embassies in Africa, twenty-eight people are dying from an explosion in Northern Ireland. In Moscow a man is swatting an old woman with a rolled-up newspaper because she pushed ahead of him in line at the bank, and salesgirls are crossing out prices with felt markers, changing the cost of apples from 10 rubles a kilo to 20 to 45. I am returning home after sixteen hours of work, and I am looking at Kevin, asleep on the couch.

I am remembering how, on the first night we made love, he felt bony and brittle. Now he is not brittle. He is bloated and soft, almost feminine, inside and out.

He rolls over and sees me staring. His eyes are yellow and bloodshot. His lips are chapped and dry.

"Did you just get in?" he says, pushing the words out with great effort. I say yes, gesturing toward my corporate casual attire. The pantyhose and the tapered navy blue skirt. The cream-colored buttoned-down shirt tucked in.

"What an insane day," I tell him, kicking off my shoes and then picking up Kesha, who has been desperately rubbing against my legs. "We filed three packages. And I lost count of the live shots. I have to go back in a few hours to help with another one for the cable show. It's a three A.M. feed."

He doesn't respond, but I continue.

"The market went nuts, did you hear?" I pour some dry food into Kesha's bowl, and he jumps from my arms, attacks it madly. "The ruble hit nine and a half to the dollar. There are already crazy lines at the banks. People trying to get their money out. To convert it to dollars before it gets worse. Did you see anything on the news?" I walk over to relieve the answering machine of its blinking red light.

"Don't bother," he mutters. "It's for me."

But it is too late. I have already pressed the button and the tape is whirring.

It's his boss from *Newsday,* back in New York. Raging that he hasn't heard from Kevin.

It's embarrassing. I stop the tape.

Kevin rolls into a fetal position, facing the back of the rose-colored sheet-covered couch.

"I guess I lost the gig," he says into the cushion.

He hasn't filed a story in days. He hasn't left the apartment in almost a week, if you don't count cigarette runs and trips to the grocery store across the street. And while he lies here, somnambulant, half-dead, the country is spinning. The ruble is crashing, the politicians are going wild. I am feeding stories to the satellite from dawn to dusk, running around shooting this tragedy, that story. Filling the air. And despite myself, despite our distillations of complicated information and convoluted situations into clipped 60-second news packages, using tired almost useless jargon and obvious footage of hysterical old women in headscarves, despite all that, I am really enjoying myself. I feel, for the first time in months, completely alive.

I say I am so sorry, and he mutters something about how it is no big deal, about how he can't bring himself to hack out their crap anyway.

He turns back to face me. "All they want is the same clichéd shit," he says. It sounds like an accusation.

185

Don't do this to me.

"There are two messages," I say. "What's the second one?"

He doesn't answer, so I play the whole tape from the start. The foreign editor, his boss, is livid. He's been running wire copy because his man in Moscow won't return his calls. Unless you are dead or hospitalized, he says, consider yourself out of a job. Beep.

Another message.

"Hey, dude, it's me. Luke." Luke says he is missing us, that he wants to come for a visit. He leaves his number and I write it down.

I turn toward the couch. Kevin is motionless, staring at the wall.

I call Luke. I beg him to come as soon as he can.

"Please come and help take care of your friend," I say. Right now, I think to myself, I cannot.

Luke says that he thinks he can leave tonight, that he can bribe the conductor for a ticket on the Krasnaya Strelka. The Red Star. It's the overnight train that arrives before most people even hit their alarms.

In the morning my alarm sounds, a shrill electronic voice calling out that it is *sem' chasov, desiat' minut.* Seven o'clock. Ten minutes. It is a talking clock, a purchase from a twenty-four-hour kiosk at the far end of Leningradsky Vokzal, Leningrad Station. Kevin bought it for me months ago, because he knew it would make me laugh. And it did, when he gave it to me. I kissed him and he kissed me back. Sweetly. Now, as I reach across him and bitterly hit the snooze bar, desperate for a few more moments of sleep, I can smell his breath. It lingers with me as I move back to my side of the bed. It is as sour as sweat, and I imagine it's adhering to the strands of my greasy, un-washed, and tangled hair.

Shit. Only fifteen minutes before Luke arrives. Recognizing that there is still nothing but a skeletal glassless frame where the bath-room's French door should be, I pull myself up to take a cold shower, making sure to turn the alarm from snooze to stop before I walk away from the bed.

The bath is the one piece of the apartment that Kolya has managed to finish properly. The enamel in the tub is clean; it feels fresh and cool under my feet. I relish turning the stainless steel knobs, which are brand new, untarnished. The showerhead is large, with a setting for massage, if you like, a gentle rinse if you don't. I close myself in behind the translucent curtain that my mother sent from Bed Bath & Beyond, a curtain still new enough to release a plastic scent when stretched across the rod, unused enough to still have creases from when it was folded in its packaging.

We still have no hot water, even though the ministry promised it weeks ago, and the pounding stream is too cold to submerge myself in, so I tilt my head back and try to dampen only my hair. Slowly, I start to wake up. One by one I soap and rinse my body's parts, trying to get myself cleaner than I have been in more than a month. And as I scrub myself with the chilled washcloth, as I soap my groin and rinse my toes, I wonder what Luke will make of this scene. I wonder what he will make of me now. I wonder if he will still think I am fabulous after I failed with his friend.

Jesus.

Have I failed? Is there something I have done to make Kevin do . . . I don't even know what. I don't even know that. I don't know what is going on or to what end. The wedding is indefinitely off. The dress was returned.

I am still wearing the ring.

I step out of the shower to look at myself.

You never know, when you are about to look in the mirror, if you are going to see yourself as others see you or if you are going to see yourself as you do. They are very different things, but perception is not something you can control, and I am always a bit surprised when I catch a glimpse of my reflection. Always. Sometimes the surprise is one of recognition, like when you are walking down the street and see an old college friend, a former teacher, maybe even a relative. Sometimes it is just shock, like you are seeing a ghost.

I step up to the mirror over the sink to see what Luke will see.

I see a ghost.

It is the ghost of the woman with a pink scarf tied around her neck and the large sunglasses precariously propped atop her head, waiting to fall to the bridge of her nose with the slightest tremor, the mildest bit of excitement or agitation. I remember her, sitting next to the minty missionary. She was hopeful, full of faith. What remains of her now is just an aura, a hint.

But I cannot say that all hope, all faith, has faded. I am still here, after all. With him. And isn't that somehow a testament of hope, a reservoir of optimism? I can't believe it is just about fear or desperation. Fear of being alone. Desperate not to be. Is it only for the job? No. I am still living with him, after all. But I can't say that I am here for the love, either. I can't say I love him anymore, because I am not sure I know what love is. Whatever I thought it was, I was clearly off-base.

I lean forward to look more closely into my eyes, as if that will provide some answers or at least give life to the phantom me. The eyes I see now have the same enlarged almond shape as they did back then, but the brown of the irises is a deeper shade, like an endless well is beneath them. Like the pupil is a pendulum that swings above a pit. Like in a story by Edgar Allen Poe.

I pick up my makeup bag from the top of the kitty litter box, which is next to the sink, and I delicately line the rims of my eyes. I put blush on my face. I paint myself presentable.

The doorbell rings, and I wrap myself in my blue terrycloth robe and go to answer it.

Luke is here, all tall and thin and bright. He has dimples and smiles and a warm hug for me the moment he comes through the door.

"How are you?" he says.

"Fine," I say, holding tightly to his broad shoulders.

He holds me back and looks at me quizzically. "How are you, really?"

I start to cry.

I start to sob. Hard. Violently. I am starting to choke. I am gasping for air to sustain the pace of the onslaught of the tears, phlegm, and snot that are darkening the gray shirt of this guy I hardly know.

"Relax," he says gently, one hand covering the back of my damp head, holding my cheek into his chest.

I don't want to relax. I want to cry and scream and carry on. I want to stay here, in these arms. I want to continue.

"Relax," he says again. "It's going to be OK."

Kevin groans from the other room, from under the sheets. "What's going on?" he says, like a moan, strained and bothered.

"Hey, man," Luke calls over my head. "Come on," he says to me, and it is OK. I pull back, still sniffling, dripping, whimpering, and I bring him to Kevin, who is prostrate, a drool stain on his pillow.

I wash my face. I reapply my mascara. I make coffee.

"What's up with this place?" Luke says, gesturing from his seat at the foot of the bed toward the bare rafters, the barren frames, the piles of construction unconstructed.

Kevin sits up and laughs. Laughs at the lunacy of it.

I laugh too and blow my nose.

I get dressed, crouching modestly behind the couch, and go off to work.

"Good luck today," says Luke as I walk to the door.

"Call and let us know when you'll be home," says Kevin.

"What?" I say, not sure I heard him correctly.

"Maybe you can meet us for dinner or something," he says.

I look wide-eyed at Luke to see if he is as shocked as I am, but he just sits there, sipping his coffee contentedly.

"OK," I say, more like a question than an affirmation.

I do call them from work, from my cell on the street while searching, with the camera crew, for signs of hysteria and destitution, for vivid illustrations of a country's decay.

"*Ia Slushaiu,*" says Kevin, answering the phone. He is alert. He is himself.

"Hi," I say, still confused. "It's me."

He asks how I am, how the story is. If I am getting good stuff, how many packages we are feeding. He asks if I am tired, if I got enough sleep, if I can meet them for dinner. And if not, if they can meet me. I say OK, too happy to have him back to question the change, the energy.

I get out at eight and they take me to Shinok, our favorite over-priced New Russian theme restaurant, the one with rows of black Mercedeses parked in front and a glass-enclosed working farm in-side. The tables surround the pastoral fantasy so that we can look at the small, wrinkled babushka picking up after the animals while we order our meal. We eat Ukrainian stew and admire the chickens. We chew Chicken Kiev and watch the horse and the goat as they chomp on their hay.

"I wonder what Tolstoy would make of this," says Kevin.

"Hell with that," I say. "She's probably getting paid better than most Muscovites."

"Yeah," says Luke. "Kevin, maybe you can get work here."

It is now an old joke but we laugh. Kevin laughs. I wonder if he would laugh if I said that.

"Luke," I say, "would you pass me the wine?"

His hand touches mine at the neck of the bottle, and in the corner of my eye I can see Kevin taking a deliberately large bite of his meal.

Later, when we are at home and Kevin is outside having a smoke, Luke touches my hand again. We are sitting on the couch, watching but not watching television.

I look at him, all healthy cheeked and California positive.

"Are you OK?" he says. I smile gently and say that with him around, for some reason, things are good. He tells me that he can tell that something is wrong, that Kevin still seems a little off, a little manic now. I say it is light-years better than he was not twenty-four hours earlier. Luke says he knows, but he also knows it is an act, that he has seen it before.

"I am just glad you're here," I say.

His large, masculine hand presses gently upon my own, which feels childlike underneath. "Glad I could come," he says.

"Maybe he just needed a friend around to snap out of it."

"I don't think it's that simple, Jen."

"But maybe it is." But, of course, it isn't. I mean, I know that. But please, please just allow me this bit of relief, this momentary respite.

"What happens when I leave?" he asks.

I take my hand away. "Excuse me," I say and go to get a glass of water.

I don't have to work on Saturday, so we hang out, the three of us. We go to a cafe, we see a movie. At the Kremlin we buy ice cream and lean on the fence surrounding Red Square. We watch as the tourists pose in front of Lenin's Tomb. They pay the man with the Polaroid for a portrait with a monkey.

Having Luke around is like having a guest in your hometown. Suddenly, through the eyes of the other, you start to see and feel things long ignored. Good things. Like how the bulbous cupolas of St. Basil's shine at the far end of the expansive, cobbled space. Like a postcard. Like the first image that came to mind when I first thought of Moscow, Moscow as an elegant, slightly exotic dream, as a mysterious, somewhat oppressive place, a place where specks of gold and color escape from the drudgery of the everyday, a hellish place that for no rational reason is eternally optimistic. You notice things like how—when talking about politics, the media, societal mores—Kevin and I can finish each other's sentences. How we laugh at the same stupid jokes. How sometimes he reaches forward and touches my hair, just on impulse.

Luke leaves on Sunday night, and we take him the station, Leningradsky Vokzal.

"Call me," he says into my ear when he kisses me on the cheek.

We wave him into the warmth of the cabin, to his lower-tier bunk that he is too long for. I want, for a moment, to join him. I want to crawl onto one of the red vinyl posts and cover myself with the dusty blanket that is folded at the end. Instead, we stand back and watch the train disappear down the dark tracks, covering our ears from the noise.

Alone, we return home, turning the lock with our comic keys, giggling about the strip of wallpaper that has fallen to the floor, kissing each other tenderly.

We hold each other when we lie in bed.

"Jen?"

"Yeah?"

We whisper.

"Luke thinks I should get more treatment."

"Yeah." I brush his stubbly cheek with the back of my hand. He looks at me, asking. "I think he is right," I answer.

He nods a little.

"But for real, you know?"

He says he does. He says, in fact, that he and Luke called his father in Minnesota to arrange for a stay in a facility run by a family friend. He says he is going to leave in a few days' time.

"What?"

"I need to do this, Jen."

I ask when they called, why they did this without me, what his father said. I ask many things, but, ultimately, the answers don't matter because he is right, he has to go. I know this, but my eyes well up with tears. I blink and knock the pooling liquid down, dripping onto Kevin, because his arm is cradling my head.

He kisses my eyelids, my forehead. "It's going to be OK," he says. He says he will be back before the fall, that it's only a six-week program.

"Yes," I am about to say, but his lips are pressing softly against mine. Sweet tongues prying lips open to dance across each other's mouth. Gentle hands feeling for the silhouette of the love we had forgotten. We move slowly, as if to make it last, to savor the sensation. It has, after all, been awhile.

I feel his fingers, their coarseness softened under the juice from my flesh, the wetness that is uncontrollable. I feel him harden against my thigh and then more so in my hand. Then he enters me and we are intertwined, inseparable.

"You feel delicious," he whispers into my ear.

But I can't say the same, because suddenly I realize that it is not Kevin I am feeling swollen, pulsing inside me. It is Luke. Luke who is actually asleep on the train right now. This thought surprises me, but somehow it also satisfies. I grab Kevin's back and pull him deeper inside.

Suddenly, he stops moving. He pulls out.

"What the fuck," he says.

"What?" Shit, I think, he knows what I'm thinking.

"Oh," he laughs, "Kesha was biting my foot." And then he kisses me, enters again. I close my eyes and reengage with my fantasy.

It is exciting: fucking and thinking that maybe Luke wants this, maybe in his mind he is joining me too. Maybe he is hard and touching himself as the train barrels toward St. Petersburg. I smile and kiss Kevin, grateful to have this moment.

We climax together.

Lying here, eyes so close that we have Cyclops vision, the excitement slowly dissipates and the fantasy dissolves. It is just us, hands intertwined and glued with sweat.

We are still, both staring at the white plaster ceiling.

"You should be with Luke," he says.

"What?" I say, not sure I heard him correctly.

"You should be with Luke. He'd be better for you."

"What are you talking about?"

"I was just thinking."

"That's ridiculous."

"You wanted him to fuck you. You said so yourself," he says.

"What?"

"You said his name when we were having sex."

Did I? "I did not," I say.

"Yes, you did."

"You're crazy."

"Don't bullshit me, Jen," he says sharply.

I should just get up and leave. I don't know why I don't. I suppose I am taking pleasure in his jealousy. Pleasure that, as I am realizing now, my possible con-coital comment had hurt him. He has hurt me so much, but because he is so delicate and capable of doing anything to himself or anyone else, I am not allowed to hurt him. I am allowed only to absorb his pain.

"Kevin," I say, breathing in the last bit of satisfaction that I can suck from this and returning to that place I have been for weeks, maybe months, now. That place where I am a punching bag into which he can release his rage so he can stay alive. "I don't think I said that. But if I did, it doesn't matter. I mean, Christ, I have had rape fantasies, but that doesn't mean I want to be raped."

He thinks about this for a minute and then says, "Good."

I don't say anything. The truth, of course, is that I do want to sleep with his friend. I want to have sex with someone else to prove to myself that I can extricate myself from this situation. Luke is the first person whose presence makes it seem possible. In an ordinary time, in an ordinary place, Luke is not the kind of guy I would fall for. But that is neither here nor there. There and here, I am lying in the bed I made in the tiny one-room apartment in the center of Moscow that we moved into a little more than four months before. Here we lie, and I change the subject.

"Have you decided what day you want to go home?"

He doesn't answer right away, so I continue.

"Because, if you could hold off until the end of the week, it would be helpful to me."

What I am thinking? Without Luke his presence will become a bigger and bigger burden. With all that is going on at work, you would think that I would want him out like yesterday. But perhaps, I think, riding on the tail of Luke's visit, we might be able to spend a few normal days together, salvage something. And besides, I have no idea how to handle Kolya the landlord; I don't want to deal with going to the special bank to pay the bills. I don't know where to go if I need this piece of information, to break that piece of red tape. I don't know how to be alone in Russia. I want to buy time.

"So, what day?" I say again, tentatively, knowing I probably shouldn't say it. I continue softly. "Because there are a lot of things we'll need to take care of before you go."

"Fuck you," he says.

"What? I just—"

"You just what?" he shouts. He is shouting at me about what, I don't know. I am shocked silent, sitting still. "You just fucking what?"

And then what? What now? The sequence of the events flies in and out my mind's focus. The chronology is lost. At what point does he throw himself out of bed and punch a hole in the kitchen wall? Is it before or after he slams the bottle of laundry detergent against the refrigerator, causing it to explode and coat half the apartment in the soapy pink mucus that will drip off the rafters for days to come? And when exactly do the ranting and raving turn from self-reflective pity into a rage against me? I honestly cannot see beyond the flashes:

Kevin is sitting on the edge of the kitchen table. Unclothed. Disconsolate. How can you be so selfish to think I could last here another day? he barks into me. You could never understand how horrible it is to be me. You will never know the sting of a mother's hand or the poison of professional failure. You cannot imagine any of it. You are a stupid, naive, innocent child. How dare you be so foolish? How dare you even try to understand?

He is sobbing in an almost inhuman timbre. I stand there naked before him and try to reach out with my shaky right hand. I want to touch him, take away some of the pain. We can share it and it will not hurt as much, I want to say. But as my arm stretches toward him, he responds with the strength of a thousand black belts, slapping my arm out of the way. Were I not familiar with the basic principles of the human form, I would say my arm is knocked like a windmill in a storm, spinning out of control and propelling me against the wall.

But it is most likely not the propeller action of my arm that tosses me into the sticky, detergent-saturated wall. It is most likely Kevin. I can't say.

I can't say at what point I run into the bathroom and slam the empty door frame, hiding behind the open crosses of wood as I frantically dial Mary's number. I hover under my terrycloth robe, cordless phone in hand, in the corner of the bathtub as if its cold porcelain walls can protect me. Is this before or after he tears the apartment key out of my hand, ripping my skin with the force of its teeth, and locks me in? It must be after. Yes, it is after. I am crying for help into a friend's finicky answering machine while his shoulder breaks down the frame. I hear Mary's voice pick up as the phone flies out of my hand.

What happens next? What happens now?

Right. I know. The phone rings and he hurls it at me. I scramble to get it off the bath mat. It's Mary. Are you OK? she asks. I can't answer because Kevin is tearing the phone from me again and throwing me out of the bathroom and into the hard steel door. You want to leave? You scared little bitch. He jams a key into the lock and flings me down the narrow piss-stained corridor. Go run, he says. Go run like the little scared selfish bitch you are. I try to run, but my path is cut off by the large slab of wood that he has thrown in my way. The wood blows wind in my face as it careens past my head. It crashes with fury against the entrance door, splintering as it lands.

Then I run.

I run faster than I have ever run. I run down the cracked cement steps and into the yard. I run barefoot through pools of mud and over scattered pipes. My blind fury trips me up and I fall, palms first, into dark musty dirt, but I don't stop. Like a sprinter at the starting block, I pull myself up and propel my body forward. And in the cool air around me I can hear an echo of what sounds like crowds cheering but must be my cry.

Mary's figure emerges from behind the large maze of pipes that separates our yards. She grabs me and hugs me and tries to get me to explain what is going on. I try to tell her, but it doesn't make sense.

"Was he drinking?" she asks.

"No," I say, "he doesn't drink."

She looks at me with disbelief and shakes her head. "Let's go up to my place, and I will make you some tea," she says, placing her arm around my shoulders and guiding me in the proper direction.

"Fuck!" I pull myself from her embrace and start running back toward my building.

"Jen! Don't! Wait!"

"He's going to do it," I say, not stopping. "Mary, he's going to do it. He's going to kill himself." I feel her hand grab at my wrist. She says something, but all I can hear is a deafening heartbeat and the sound of pouring blood.

She stops me. Redirects me.

We run to the street and wave down a police car. Mary, breathless, explains the situation to the two officers, and we beg for them to accompany us back to my apartment.

"That's not our department," says the cop in the passenger seat. His partner is too busy sucking on a Byelomore cigarette to respond.

"Her fiancé might be dying in there!" Mary points in the direction of the apartment. "And you are just going to sit here, smoking your fucking cigarette?" The cops look at us with steady, cold eyes. "Call *nul'-dva*," they say. Zero-two, Moscow's 911. "It's not our department."

And then I start to laugh. Hysterically. A hard, horrendous hyena laugh. "There aren't any working phones anywhere near here," I manage to say. I am laughing so hard that mucus sprays out of my nose. I wipe it off my face with the sleeve of my bathrobe and laugh some more.

"Come on," says Mary. She leads me back to her apartment where she tries to call my apartment to make sure Kevin is still alive.

The line is busy.

"He could have just knocked it off the hook," I say, wrapping a kitchen towel around my bleeding feet.

We think about calling the police again but rule that out when I remember that neither Kevin nor I have bothered to register in

Moscow. A rumor was going around about some GAI, some city police, who beat the living shit out of an unregistered foreigner while they raped his girlfriend. If you aren't registered, you don't exist. Sometimes that's safer, but if you don't exist, it doesn't matter what they do to you.

"Well, if he hasn't successfully killed himself, there's nothing like a few drunk *militsionery* to finish the job," says Mary.

"And then they would steal my laptop."

"And slaughter your cat."

"How about an ambulance?" I say.

"They have to report all calls to the police," she says. We call my house again. The line is still busy.

We call Mikhail and Ostap. We call all our male acquaintances. No one is home. No one can come help.

We call the American Medical Center, but they won't serve us without a credit card number.

"Do you think she took her wallet when she was running for her life?" Mary yells into the phone before slamming it down.

And then we call his mother.

24

Lying in me, as though it were a white
Stone in the depths of a well, is one
Memory that I cannot, will not, fight:
It is happiness, and it is pain.
Anyone looking straight into my eyes
Could not help seeing it, and could not fail
To become thoughtful, more sad and quiet
Than if he were listening to some tragic tale.
I know the gods changed people into things,
Leaving their consciousness alive and free.
To keep alive the wonder of suffering,
You have been metamorphosed into me.

      Anna Akhmatova (1889–1966)

Moscow —Which is more upsetting, an attack on your body or an assault on your mind? Is it worse to have your wrist slapped and your feet bloodied, or is having all trust obliterated more painful?

"You should stay away from him when he gets like this," my once future mother-in-law says to me when I call. "He can be violent sometimes."

She knows this now and she knew it before, when she was hugging me in Manhattan, when she told me she loved me like a daughter. "You are family," she said back then, and I realize that in some ways, it's still the same. Family to her is something that can be cast away. Family can be someone else's problem. Her son is my problem. It is my problem to figure out what to do, how to calm him down, how to get him to Minnesota. It is my problem to make sure he is safe.

I suppose immortality is easy if, like Rebecca Dillard, you act like you don't really exist in the first place, like you don't register.

But I do exist. I can feel the cuts on my feet, each gasping to fight off infection. I can feel the rawness of the skin on my wrist, inflamed from escaping the grasp of a maddened claw. I can feel the fear in my parents' voices when I call them. I can feel the pain of my heart, breaking.

It is daybreak now, Monday morning, five o'clock. I watch from Mary's window how the dew sprinkles over the mud and the pipes in our yard, making it look somehow magical and kind. From here I can see the front door to my building. It is open wide, probably because I was the last one to leave.

We did go back, of course, because he could have been dead.

We entered slowly, at about 3 A.M., me shuffling in Mary's shoes, Mary wearing her trench coat like a detective, collar up, both of us moving with delicate, quiet strides.

"Kevin?"

He didn't answer, but I could see him, asleep on the bed. The street lamp from the yard illuminated his face. He looked wet, almost. Glistening, like he was sweating. As I got closer I could see that his eyelids were twitching. They fluttered so hard that it seemed they should be making a noise, like the sound of a fly getting electrocuted. But there was silence, except for his breathing, which was heavy and almost guttural, like a sleeping bear. I went farther into the apartment to gather some clothes, my cell phone, the laptop, and the cat. Mary stood guard at the door, ready to, well, do something if need be. Then we left. And that was that.

And now here I am, sitting in her kitchen, looking at my door. I guess I am waiting for the cell to ring or the doorbell to sound or to wake up from this dream. It is a dream, not a fantasy.

Nothing happens, but somehow, gradually, the day emerges. I manage to shower and get dressed. I call my office and tell them I am sick. I call his father's friend in Wisconsin and arrange for the intake. I go to the airline office and charge a ticket to my credit card. Round-trip, because it is cheaper than one-way. I call Kolya, the landlord, because I know he can help. He escorts me to the apartment to pack Kevin up. Kevin lies in bed, a puffy, slimy, six-foot-long piece of flesh. He tries to speak but is incoherent. Kolya folds him into the car and takes him to the airport. And then it is night again, and Kesha and I return to our bed.

One week passes. And then two and then three. Yeltsin fires another prime minister. The ruble continues to plummet. President Clinton comes to town. Back in the States, Kevin runs away from rehab, and then, after three days of being missing in action, turns up at his mother's house in Massachusetts. From there he calls me repeatedly, desperate and pleading and tremendously sad. I repeatedly call his mother, arguing for hours about reimbursement for the ticket, the phone calls, the repairs to the door that Kevin broke on the night of his rage. She tells me that it is my responsibility, the approximately $2,000 is my burden to bear.

I go through this all, my life, in slow motion, keeping it cool, keeping things in line. When people ask, I say he is home because of his appendix. I say things are fine, but the wedding is postponed. I don't say it's over, not even to myself. Which, I suppose, is a curious thing.

My family says that if I take him back, they will love me, but they won't recognize the couple I am part of. It will not exist, with or without documentation. They are able to have some of the deposit on the inn reimbursed. They beg me to come home, to make sure I am in New York before Kevin returns to Moscow. I imagine walking down Broadway and bumping into an old friend; I imagine that typical "what's up?" conversation, and I know I can't face it. I can't face the people who will say, "I told you so." I can't give them the satisfaction. Or maybe I just don't want to admit that they were right. I want to believe that I did the right thing, chasing my fantasy, chasing this unknown. I still believe, I really do, that maybe if he comes back, it would be OK. We could live apart and then just take it slow, reestablish things with pacing and time and patience. My aunt, who is also a therapist, calls and tells me that it is typical for abused women to think that things are fixable. But I am not an abused woman, not really. And I hear in his voice (transmitted from a pay phone in the cold corridor of an institution) that he wants to change. I want to give him a reason to continue wanting.

"I got a diagnosis," he tells me one night as I am lying in bed, scratching the back of Kesha's ears.

"What do you mean?"

"Manic depression, I guess. Bipolar disorder. They are putting me on lithium," he says.

I hadn't even considered this as an option, that his behavior was diagnosable, but I suppose it makes sense. In a way, it is comforting. His insanity wasn't just drug-induced madness; his violence was beyond his control. I once read a memoir about a woman living with manic depression, *An Unquiet Mind,* by Kay Redfield Jamison, and I recall how much the lithium helped her, how even though the demons remained, she was functional. And married. And now, slowly, I can hear him returning to lucidity. I can feel the old sepia-toned warmth and the quirky charisma. The support. He tells me from thousands of miles whom to call for the story, what angle to take. He helps me when I get an assignment to write an article for a glossy American men's magazine. I e-mail the text and he edits it before I send it to the editors. Sometimes I take his advice. Sometimes I don't. And as the articles pile up and the television segments calm down, as the weather gets colder and days get shorter, I start to get a bit more lucid too.

"You aren't coming back, are you?" I say after he has postponed his return flight for the fourth time.

"Not for another month," he says. "I need a little more time."

It is October now, and the chill in the air starts to get under my skin. Moscow is starting to feel more like a cliché again, gray and bitter. The collapse of the ruble has created a mood more dour, an atmosphere more tense. My girlfriends and I work it off by going to seedy nightclubs and dancing on tables, behaving in ways that I never would at home. I live my life outside myself, never thinking, never crying, never mourning the loss of things. I buy time and pay no mind to my future. Instead, I write funny articles for magazines and I kiss strange men in bars. I start to live my fantasies.

"The lights pan over the glistening body of the male stripper; his family jewels are safely encased in a gold-sequined G-string. Teenage girls have packed themselves against the stage in numbers that would break any U.S. fire-code regulations—but this is Moscow, and there are no such restraints," I write for *Maxim* magazine.

"Shake it, Sergei!" the D.J. barks in English, and the glittering Adonis hauls a girl out of the audience and onto the stage. In one swift movement, he rips off her blouse and starts sucking one of her breasts to the beat. When another dancer struts out, many in the audience have to be physically restrained to keep them from offering themselves up for sacrifice.

Just another ladies' night at the Hungry Duck. Here's how it works. Three times a week, the doors open at 7 p.m. to any girl who's 18 or older and willing to fork over 10 rubles—about 60 cents. Inside, the potent mix of Chippendales-style dancers and endless free drinks drives women into a state of rapture.

Outside, a testosterone-laden army of men piles up and pays about 6 percent of their monthly salaries for the right to barge in the moment the ladies-only festivities are over and take advantage of the boozed-up sea of female flesh within. Expatriate American men boast of having to walk no farther than the front door before they're forced to peel drunk, insatiably horny girls off them. I let my girlfriends talk me into a night at the notorious Duck. I thought, What the hell: I'm here, I might as well see what the fuss is about.

The Hungry Duck is one metro stop from the Kremlin, kitty-corner to the old KGB headquarters. At the door, a Notorious B.I.G.-size guard—with a breadbox-size gun cradled like a baby in his arms—stopped us and said he'd have to undress us to confirm that we were in fact female. None of us knew how to respond; he did have that gun. But after a moment of unsteady silence, we just smiled and walked in. We were early, so we scored a good scoping table and watched as hundreds of girls oozed in to fight over the stools just outside the large ring-shaped bar, where a high table served as the stage for the debauchery to come.

It was like a bad sorority movie: With their halter tops and skin-tight pants, sheer shirts and mini-miniskirts, these girls were ready for a night of . . . well, something.

FOREPLAY

The D.J. started spinning hormonally charged, sexy dance music, and the sea of girls started getting drunk fast. Before an hour had gone by, everyone was dancing, grinding, and what have you. Yes, we got into it, too: I was up on the bar with my girlfriends, impro-vising the lambada and bumping butts. No offense, but I can't ex-plain the thrill and freedom I felt, having no men around. It was great. Hundreds of girls, half-dressed and dancing like mad and not giving a damn what they looked like. We were just a happy, sweaty sisterhood.

THE ACT

At eight o'clock, the lights suddenly dimmed, and everyone excit-edly scattered back to the stools and tables they'd claimed earlier in the evening. And the striptease began.

The five dancers were pretty impressive-looking: I later found out they're among the highest-paid models in Moscow. But I just didn't get it; personally, I really don't see the sexiness in gold-sequined G-strings. The rest of the crowd, however, seemed more than pleased. The pixie blonde beside me nearly burst my eardrum when "Andrei" ran a thumb along his waistband.

"*Da! Da!*" she cried, and Andrei tossed a pelvic thrust at her.

THE CLIMAX

After about 20 minutes of gyrations, the dancers began picking girls to bring into their act, and the action really started heating up.

Girls begged to be pulled onto the stage, where they were systematically stripped, licked, and fondled by the hands and tongues of the dancers for all the crowd to see and cheer. Cunnilingus was the least of it: It was an absolute Roman orgy going on up there, with half-naked girls mauling these dancers, and vice versa, to the throbbing beat of the music. It was too dark to see, but there may well have been de facto fucking going on.

THE POSTCOITAL SMOKE

After a solid hour of stripping and licking and dry humping and lord knows what else, the Hungry Duck let in the guys who'd massed around the gates like sperm outside an egg.

And yes, I suppose if I were a horny man who just wanted to have no-strings-attached sex, I'd pay more or less whatever it cost to get in. My God. But I'd fill an extra suitcase with condoms. AIDS is on the rise, syphilis is epidemic, and crabs crawl freely from St. Petersburg to Vladivostok.

I wandered away from a lusty Canadian and his miniskirted girl and watched another woman make her way down an aisle, French-kissing four guys along the way.

Must be something in the vodka.

For *New York Magazine* I write a profile of a Newark native who, as a DJ, is the hottest ticket in town. I sell another story about Matryoshka dolls stacked with all of Clinton's lovers. I pander in gently masked smut. I am the third person described in my scenes.

It isn't why I came here, but for now it feels oddly like a reason to stay. The praise starts coming, both for the articles and the packaged sensationalism (Death! Destruction! Destitution!) I send over the network airways, and suddenly the network is proposing a staff position, complete with benefits and stability. They offer to fly me home to meet with the staff in New York, and I think that with this endorsement, I might be able to face the crowds on the street.

Kevin, who is now just an outpatient at the institution, says he will pick me up at the airport. He says he can borrow his latest stepfather's car.

"You won't be able to come up to my parents' apartment," I say.

"I know," he says, "but it would be nice to see you." He asks me to bring some of his things, to bring his cat.

So I pay a hundred dollars for a vet to come over and falsify papers to prove Kesha has been vaccinated, which he hasn't been, and I fold Kevin's shirts and underwear into tight little squares. I ask the office manager at the bureau to make me a reservation.

She gets me a ticket for October 31.

"Oh, my God," I say.

"What?"

I don't tell her that was supposed to be my wedding day.

What do you put on when you wake up in the morning of the day you aren't getting married? What do you wear when you are going to cross an ocean with an increasingly incontinent cat? How do you prepare yourself for a journey that moves against the clock, like it is meant to erase time? Am I the opposite of those trafficked girls that brought me here last winter, free to come and go, totally unattached? Or am I like them in some way, stuck in some warp that I can't comprehend? These thoughts flutter through my mind, but I don't answer them. Instead, I have Elena pick me up in the morning. She helps me drug Kesha with a bit of crushed Valium and drag all the bags to the airport. She negotiates with the customs official as he examines my slightly suspect pet. She escorts me to passport control and kisses me on my cheek.

"Are you coming back?" she says.

"Of course, silly," I say. "I'll be back in a week. I live here."
I have to.

"What a cute cat," the woman seated next to me says as I try to shove the carrying case under the seat in front of me. "What's his name?"

"Kesha," I say, in a tone to suggest I don't want to chat, but she doesn't get it.

"Are you moving back to the States?"

I look at her, this woman in a peach-colored twin sweater set with overly frosted blond hair. An American, probably from the Midwest. She is wide-eyed and seems enthusiastic. Her perfume smells like the main floor of Bloomingdale's.

"Just him," I say pointing to the box that holds the cat. "I'm helping him emigrate." And then, despite myself, I engage her a little. "He even has a passport. Here." I hold back my hair as I fumble through my knapsack to pull out the glossy card with his certifications.

She looks at it and laughs and tells me, apropos of nothing, that she was in Moscow on business, that she works for a pharmaceutical company. I smile and, when asked, just say I am a writer. She sees my ring and asks if my fiancé lives in Moscow too.

"Sometimes," I say and close my eyes to approximate sleep.

I am awakened by a stinging sensation inside my nasal membranes. A sharp stench, like a combination of a urine-soaked train and a wet hamper filled with gym clothing, is emanating from under my feet. The woman has moved across the aisle, and when she sees that I am awake, she looks at me and rolls her eyes. Pinching my nose, I look down at Kesha through the holes in his cage. He is cowering in the back corner, terrified. He sees me and whines.

And then there is that beep, to please fasten your seat belts and prepare for landing. We are arriving in Helsinki for a one-hour layover, for coffee and fuel.

I run through the sterile, squeaky clean passenger waiting area, past the espresso bar, directly to the white-tiled ladies' room, where I—dressed in my wedding day jeans and white Nordic sweater—try to shower the cat in the smooth metal sink. I clean out the interior of the piss-soaked cage. Water sprays everywhere as Kesha fights madly from under my grasp. The other women, trying to brush their teeth, apply makeup, or just wash their hands, are shaking their heads, cursing me with their eyes.

"I am already cursed," I say under my breath as I try to dry the wet, mangy beast with the brown paper towels someone, I don't know who, has handed to me.

I force Kesha back into his cage and lock the latch with a satisfaction I haven't felt in awhile. I look in the mirror. I look like him, I think. Like them. Like Kevin and his cat; hair sticking out all over the place, sweater dirty, wet, and torn at the sleeve. Tired, bloodshot eyes, lined with wrinkles, not from smiling. I take a deep breath and wash my face. I mop up the mess that I have made of the sink but leave the puddles on the floor to someone who is paid to take care of such things. My head starts pounding, like there is a chainsaw hacking through my brain. Slowly. Gingerly. With great care and deliberation. It is tearing through, millimeter by millimeter, as if it were carving out each individual synapse, every single cell.

I take the last codeine I have and, with the cat clean, reboard the plane.

The light goes bing.

And as I emerge from behind the customs fence, I see him.

I see him, and I don't know whether to laugh or to cry.

He is fatter now. Fat. The now-rounded jaw is framed by a short, undernourished beard that is bald in places, solid in others, unclear what color it wants to be, whether it should be curly or straight. It looks like pubic hair growing back after a bad wax job. His glasses are still dirty, his jacket still unwashed. His jeans look like they have been dragged through the mud.

He was supposed to be in a tuxedo.

"Hey," he says, giving me a big long hug. "It's so good to see you."

"Yeah," I say and hand him the cage with the cat.

I walk next to the man I had once committed my life to, but as we reach for his bags coming around the carousel, as I watch this man who might be mistaken for a bum reach for the tattered gray army surplus knapsack that I had packed for him, the same bag that once hid a vodka bottle from my sight, I find myself imagining an emotional loophole. The man I committed myself to doesn't really exist. There is probably even documentation to prove it.

"You look great," he says to me as we push the cart toward the automatic doors and out into the crisp autumn air.

I laugh. "Now I know I can never trust what you say."

He laughs too, because apparently enough time has passed to allow this to happen. Tragedy plus time, and all that. Ha. Ha.

The Ford Explorer is set up for Kesha, with a litter pan and a cushion in the back. Kevin takes him out of the case, snuggles with him briefly, and then lets the cat stretch his legs. Kevin also has brought an opened bag of premium cat food and a toy on a string.

"That was thoughtful of you," I say, nodding at the arrangement.

"Only the best for my buddy."

Yeah, I know. "Oh," I say and hand him the kitty passport, the falsified documents, the medical bill.

He crumples them into his pocket and we climb into the car.

We drive but we don't really speak. It is not for me to entertain him with tales from his rejected land. It is not the time for him to tell me what has happened, what has gone through his mind. Instead, he peppers the silence with occasional questions, asked awkwardly. Have you heard from Kolya? Is the apartment still a mess? How's Elena? (Not like he cares.) He tells me that he has set up a painting studio in his mother's garage. That he spends his days drenched in oils and it feels great. I ask if he has found any work, what he is doing for money, but he says he's not ready yet, he can't go there.

"I hate to ask this," I say, "but I really need that money. You know, for the plane and all that." I don't mention the money lost on the wedding, the thousands of dollars that I had to cover for the rent.

"I know," he says. "I feel horrible about it and want to repay you." He shifts forward in his seat and pulls a crinkled white envelope from the back pocket of his jeans. "Here, it's a start."

I open the envelope, which had been licked and sealed and clearly thought through. Inside is a rumpled twenty-dollar bill.

"I can't take this," I say and give it back to him.

"Why not? It's a start."

"Pay me when you can pay me for real."

We are quiet for a moment.

"Why don't you give me the ring," he says. "I can pawn it."

I look at it, the tiny diamonds, the beaten facets, and I remove it from my wedding finger. "I don't think it is worth that much," I say, and I put it on my thumb. "And, anyway, it's mine."

We pass through the working-class suburban towns and approach the city, the skyline pulling us in. I have this feeling that I should feel comfort in the familiar, but I don't. I don't feel much of anything.

"Do you know today was supposed to be our wedding day?" I say as we drive up to my parents' door.

"It was?"

We are silent for a moment.

"You know what? I will take that twenty."

There was really nothing else to say.

And so it goes. I meet with the suits and see some friends. Everyone is kind, everyone is glad to see me, to see that I am OK. No one says I told you so.

I have lunch with a men's magazine editor who offers more work. I meet the evening show's famous anchor, knowing he will never remember that we have met. I visit Ivan, my cat, who is still living in my sublet place.

I go back to Moscow and it gets colder. We have fewer stories to produce because the home office is stuck on the Lewinsky affair and can't be bothered with foreign news. The staff job offer stalls out with no sign of reignition. Kolya has made no progress on the apartment, so I rent a room from a family off Mayakovsky Square, even closer to the Kremlin. The ruble's collapse has decimated the expat scene, and many of my party-going comrades have left or are leaving. My Russian friends continue to receive salaries in salmon, if they receive anything at all. The Starbucks supply that I brought from New York runs out and the local coffee tastes horrid.

One morning in late November I wake up and look in the mirror.

I see myself, not the ghost or the fun-house reflection. I see Jennifer, a young woman who has some regrets but who remains fairly confident about the future.

I am in Russia, I think. And not because I have to be.

I can go home.

Acknowledgments

With the rare exceptions (weddings, book acknowledgments), a person has few opportunities to express deeply felt gratitude in a public forum. I find myself tremendously lucky. Of course, because I have changed names in the book to protect identities, I must shield some of those identities here. So, to my family (my parents, my brother, my sister-in-law, and my beautiful nieces—you all know who you are)—thank you for all the good things imaginable. And to Jan Trasen, who is included under that "family" umbrella. Julie Ziegler, Jennifer Howze, and Liza Vasilkova: You each define the word *friend*. To Kevin, even though that is not really his name, for better and for worse, I am grateful.

The book part of the story would never have happened without the unfailing encouragement of Tori Rowan and the gang in her writing workshop. My agent, Stephanie Kip Rostan, brilliantly massaged the original manuscript so that when the University of Wisconsin Press's Raphael Kadushin picked it up, he didn't put it down. And with Raphael's sage guidance, the narrative really began to flow. Thank you for innumerable reasons to the following list of incredible people: Tula Karras, Carol Gilligan, Sadie Van Gelder, Carol Story, Dan McGirt, Elizabeth Shreve, Polly Kummel, Jenny Trewartha, and, finally, to Michael Oko, who has made the real-life epilogue honestly wonderful.